MW01284720

Covenant
Divorce
and
Putting Away

Vern Peltz

**What Most Christians Don't Know About
Divorce and Remarriage,
But The Bible Has Been Saying It The Whole Time.**

Covenant, Divorce, and Putting Away

Copyright © 2017 by Vern Peltz. All rights reserved.
No part of this publication may be reproduced, stored in a retrieval system or transmitted in any way by any means, electronic, mechanical, photocopy, recording or otherwise without the prior permission of the author except as provided by USA copyright law.

Scripture quotations marked (AMP) are taken from the Amplified Bible, Copyright © 1954, 1958, 1962, 1964, 1965, 1987 by The Lockman Foundation. Used by permission.

Scripture quotations marked (KJV) are taken from the Holy Bible, King James Version, Cambridge, 1769. Used by permission. All rights reserved.

Scripture quotations marked (NIV) are taken from the Holy Bible, New International Version®, NIV®. Copyright © 1973, 1978, 1984 by Biblica, Inc.™ Used by permission of Zondervan. All rights reserved worldwide. www.zondervan.com

Quotation of material taken from The Works of Josephus, The Whiston translation online. Copyright © 1998-2010 G. J. Goldberg. All rights reserved. http://www.josephus.org/

Contents

Introduction

Divorce is devastating to everyone who goes through it. It affects lives in horrific ways. I personally don't know of anyone who has gone through a divorce who felt the process was a good experience. It can leave the divorcees with long-term scars, bad memories, and pain that doesn't go away easily.

The American institutions of family and marriage are facing critical times. At the time this book was written, statistically we saw fewer divorces taking place than, let's say, 30 years ago (most statistics are currently placing the divorce rate between 40-50%). Even at that percentage, it still basically amounts to a coin toss as to whether a marriage will last or not.

We live in a time of history where the institution of marriage is being challenged from many sides. Man to man, and woman to woman unions (same-sex marriages) are in the process of receiving legal recognition and endorsement. There is also the advent of what is being referred to as "Starter Marriages". These are marriages in which the couple is learning how to make marriage type of relationships work. From the onset, they are not really expected to last. If they do, that's good. However, if they fail, hopefully lessons will be learned that can be carried on to the next marriage. The idea is that the next marriage is more apt to survive because of what was learned in the first one. This is all besides the masses of people who are not married, but still living together as if they were.

Then there are the millions of married couples who struggle with their relationship on a daily basis. The happiness, contentment, satisfaction, and hope are gone. It has become an on-going battle of pain, insults, tears, anger, resentment, and desperation to even hold on another day. Abuse piles on top of abuse. Bitterness, resentment, and unforgiveness become bedfellows, and before long, the "pain" of going on in this situation becomes too much for the "gain" that it offers. The dreaded papers are served. It's another divorce.

Yet in many cases, going through the actual divorce is not the most difficult aspect of it. No matter what the circumstances, it is often the proceeding condemnation and rejection from family, friends, and acquaintances that leaves the divorcee more devastated than the actual divorce proceedings.

Too often this happens for the cause of righteousness and believers trying to hold a righteous standard for marriage. Long-standing friendships are broken. Distrust is born that often grows and endures for years or even lifetimes. In the church community, those who have gone through it are often shunned or made to feel very uncomfortable in certain circles of people or settings. The sad part is: most of the time the people involved don't even have a good understanding of what the Bible really says about the subject. They think they do, but in reality, they don't. As a result, many divorcees are mishandled by the church. Since it is such a large part of the population, it would behoove the Christian community to learn how to deal with these people in a more effective manner if we are going to influence our world.

The purpose of this book is to offer some insight into God's perspective on this whole thing. Since He's the one who invented the marriage relationship, it may be worth seeing the framework in which He had intended it to function.

We will be looking at the following three inter-related, yet distinctly different subjects:

Covenant, Putting Away, and Divorce.

1.) To bring a clear, scriptural understanding to the subject of covenant, and in doing so, hopefully help some marriages be preserved and improved.

2.) To help lift the guilt and condemnation that many believers carry because they have gone through a divorce when they don't have a clear understanding of what God says about what happened in their life.

3.) And lastly, to give some insight into the subjects of divorce and re-marriage according to what the Bible actually says about them. Again, I repeat something I said earlier: many believers think they know what the Bible says about divorce and remarriage, but as you read this book, you may find it's a little different than you thought, as well as why it's different than the traditional church view-point.

I have hesitated to write this book for many years. The reason I haven't done it is because of the people who may try to use this material as an excuse to get a divorce. That's not my purpose for this book. Scriptural-ly speaking, marriage is a relationship that needs to be preserved far before many others. It was intended by God that marriage is to last a lifetime.

Yet God is not happy with what happens in many marriages. The abuse, rejection, fear, pain, etc. that plague many marriages on a daily basis is not what God designed the institution of marriage to be. I find myself being confronted on a continual basis with the reality that there are many, many deeply hurting people in this world who have been devas-tated through a bad marriage. On top of that problem, the church

-- which is to support healing, health, and righteousness in bad marriage situations -- too many times only drives the pain of a failed marriage deeper into the person. Our traditions, rules, criticism, "holier-than-thou" attitudes, shaming, shunning, legalism, and judgmental approach to helping someone usually only proves one thing -- we don't understand God's heart on this subject and therefore can't show it to the people who are suffering or have suffered a divorce.

I know this can be a very sensitive subject with many people. That sensitivity causes emotions to heat up, which never helps us to look at a subject or situation logically and objectively. So I am asking that you determine from the beginning of this book to make an effort to lay any emotional bias to the side and simply see what God has to say about the subject, and why He says it.

Hopefully some clarity can be brought to this very misunderstood subject.

Thank you for reading this book.

Explanation

Writers like to use various translations of the Bible. I predominantly use the King James Version (KJV), New International Version (NIV), and the Amplified Version (AMP). I realize there are many other translations available, and I'm not saying one is better than another. Let me explain my approach to the translations.

ALL Bible translations trace their origins back to the same Hebrew and Greek Manuscripts. The thing that makes them read differently has to do largely with the specific word the translators chose to represent what they were reading in the manuscripts, as well as the specific meaning to a word they chose when they translated it. When we take the time to look up the definitions in the Greek and Hebrew, we find there are many shades of meaning in a single word. The translator has to choose which one he or she feels is the most accurate and fits the context the best.

When dealing with this subject, the King James Version is one of the more accurate in its translation of the words "put away" and "divorce". For that reason, I made it the predominate translation used in this book. I used the New International Version because it is translated to fit our language style more easily than the KJV. There are many translations to choose from to help us with this issue, I chose the NIV. The last translation I used was the Amplified Version. Even though the AMP can be quite "wordy", it emphasizes the meanings to various words quite well.

The AMP amplifies the specific words by giving many of the definitions that are tied to that specific word in the scripture. As a result, we get a broader view of what a word or phrase is saying.

Often I will give some of the definitions from the Hebrew or Greek for a specific word. Please remember: that definition is from the original word of the manuscript that is being translated. Therefore it applies to every translation we may be using. So whether we're using the NKJV, Wuest, YLT, WBS, ASV, RSV, or Confraternity Version, etc. - they all trace their roots back to the same manuscripts and the same original Hebrew or Greek words. If you are wondering about the version of the Bible you use, and if it's better than other translations, the answer is this: *All Bible Translations are translated from the same original Hebrew and Greek manuscripts and words.* As a result, *all English versions of the Bible are translated from the Hebrew and Greeks words to which I am referring in this book.* If your version reads differently, it's not because the original manuscripts from which it was translated are any different or more accurate. It reads differently because that's how the translators chose to translate the specific words to which I am referring. *When I refer to a Hebrew or Greek word, it applies to your Bible -- no matter what translation you are using. All the translations are taken from the same source.*

If you are using a paraphrase Bible, even though it makes very easy reading, I would suggest you lay it to the side when you engage in in-depth study. A paraphrase simply translates the concept or feel of the verse, rather than the direct translation of the original words. Doctrinally, when compared to the original manuscripts, many paraphrase Bibles are very inaccurate in how they convey what a phrase or passage is saying. This causes a lot of confusion when those "loosely translated" thoughts are brought into the arena of intense Bible study and interpretation. For study purposes, it's best to stay with a translation, not a paraphrase.

Here's the reason I bring that up: when we are looking at the subject of divorce, it is extremely important we know which Hebrew and Greek words are being used when a scripture is dealing with the subject. Being able to grasp the subject with clarity -- or struggling in complete confusion -- has a lot to do with the original words being used. Here's the issue: not all the translators correctly translated the original words. In fact in many translations, the word "divorce" is the only word used to describe the dissolution of a marriage. As you read through this book, you will find that to be incorrect. That's what has caused a lot of the problem in understanding the subjects of divorce and remarriage.

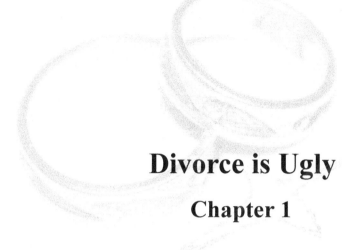

Divorce is Ugly

Chapter 1

The subject of divorce as it pertains to Christians is, at the very best, controversial. At its worst, it can be very divisive. Even though this should not be, it is. Let me say from the beginning -- this book is not designed to cause division. This book is merely a very scriptural look at something that is a huge problem in society and the Christian Church in America. Try to be objective and open-minded with the material, and please do not let the Word of God be stripped of its power and effect by your personal religious beliefs and traditions (Matthew 15:1-9; Esp. v. 6).

The purpose for writing this book is three-fold:

1.) Our goal is to develop on what the "covenant" is and what it's to look like.

2.) This will show how the aspect of divorce that God becomes very disturbed about is directly tied to breaking the covenant of the marriage. God hates "putting away" (Malachi 2:16).

3.) Lastly we need to understand that "divorce" (the legal paperwork and separation of the couple) isn't even really the issue with God. It's merely the result of one partner "putting away" the other through breaking the "covenant".

No matter how you look at a divorce, it is a very ugly thing. It leaves a lot of pain and wreckage in its wake. Adults are violated, children are decimated, finances are often destroyed -- on and on the list can go. It affects everyone touched by it, including personal and extended families, churches, and even society. Divorce always has some very unpleasant consequences that follow it. Divorce should be avoided if at all possible. I agree with what Jesus said on the subject:

Matthew 19:4-6 (NIV)
Haven't you read," he replied, "that at the beginning the Creator 'made them male and female,'and said, 'For this reason a man will leave his father and mother and be united to his wife, and the two will become one flesh'? So they are no longer two, but one. Therefore what God has joined together, let man not separate.

It is obvious what God's intent is for marriage. It's not to end in a divorce.

> ### *No matter how you look at a divorce, it is a very ugly thing.*

Now, get ready for my next statement: even though it is extremely ugly, it is something that in certain cases absolutely needs to take place. It's not God's best plan for mankind, but because sin has gotten into the human race and has caused so much devastation, there are times divorce is necessary and is actually more Godly than the alternative. In fact, you will find out there are times divorce is God's solution.

God does not view everything from just a single perspective. In other words, not everything has to be done just one way with God. There is a best way for every person, and then there are also alternatives that may not be the best, but God is still OK with them.

Romans 12:2 (AMP - underline added)
[2] Do not be conformed to this world (this age), [fashioned after and adapted to its external, superficial customs], but be transformed (changed) by the [entire] renewal of your mind [by its new ideals and its new attitude], so that you may prove [for yourselves] what is the good and acceptable and perfect will of God, even the thing which is good and acceptable and perfect [in His sight for you].

What is God saying? He's giving us some good news here. He's saying that this thing of living for Him is not "all or nothing", where we either get it all correct, or we might as well give up because we no longer measure up. God is willing to work with us even when we are not perfect! And the awesome part is that it is still all His will for us.

The older I get, the more I realize that (besides Jesus) I don't think there is one person on earth who has lived a perfect life. Everybody has messed up someplace. So, for anybody who thinks his or her life is the standard of perfection -- maybe you need to look again. We're imperfect beings, and as a result we live imperfect lives. In some way, every human being has messed up and is still messing up.

Romans 3:23 (KJV)
[23] For all have sinned, and come short of the glory of God;

1John 1:7-10 (NIV)
[7] But if we walk in the light, as he is in the light, we have fellowship with one another, and the blood of Jesus, his Son, purifies us from all sin.

[8] If we claim to be without sin, we deceive ourselves and the truth is not in us. [9] If we confess our sins, he is faithful and just and will forgive us our sins and purify us from all unrighteousness. [10] If we claim we have not sinned, we make him out to be a liar and his word has no place in our lives.

Everyone has sinned, and everyone is still sinning. The awesome part is that God understands that and is willing to work with us in spite of it.

Here's a piece of good news: your marriage situation may not fit the "perfect will of God", but that's not the end of it. There is still the "good will of God" and the "acceptable will of God", and they are all still the "will of God for you". Life on this fallen planet is not fair, and things happen that we never planned nor intended, but God will walk through all of it with us. He will not abandon us, leave us, nor forsake us. That's the perspective of a loving God.

Here is a scripture that says just that:

Hebrews 13:4-6 (NIV)
[4] Marriage should be honored by all, and the marriage bed kept pure, for God will judge the adulterer and all the sexually immoral. [5] Keep your lives free from the love of money and be content with what you have, because God has said, "Never will I leave you; never will I forsake you." [6] So we say with confidence, "The Lord is my helper; I will not be afraid. What can man do to me?"

This set of scriptures is almost ironic. Look at this with me: in verse 4 it talks about marriage and keeping it sexually pure. In verse five it talks about money and learning to be content with what we have. Then after those two statements, God say: He will never leave nor forsake us. Do you realize that He just stated two of the top issues of marriages with problems: sexual issues and money problems? God is saying, "I'll stick with you through your marriage problems and through your financial problems." Then there is verse six, which says, "Since God is with me in marriage and financial difficulties, I will not be afraid of people. What can they do to me?"

I don't think it's a coincidence that the Holy Spirit put that section of scripture together that way. Why would I say that? Because if a person gets divorced (which touches both the sexual and financial realm), God will not leave or forsake them, but many people in the church sure will! God flat out says, "Don't be afraid of them, I'll stick with you through the whole thing."

Christians can be very critical, arrogant, mean, and judgmental. I realize all of society can be that way, but as believers, we're supposed to be different. Yet many times, it's the Christians who treat the divorced person (or divorced and remarried) the worst. It's like they have become a blemish on our spotless white reputation, as if they've embarrassed us or brought shame on us somehow. It's really sad, because when the person is going through a horrific time in their life, the

> *Christians can be very critical, arrogant, mean, and judgmental. I realize all of society can be that way, but as believers, we're supposed to be different.*

people who should be there to help support and encourage are often the ones who damage that person the most. There is an old saying: "There is only one army that kills their wounded: it's the church." When it comes to the topic of divorce, that is absolutely true in too many cases.

19

Somehow believers and the church have divided sin up into categories. Some categories are "worse" than others, so we classify sin accordingly. Some sin is absolutely despicable, while other sin is quite acceptable, and most believers participate. (For example: I personally have observed lying / deceit and gossip to be sins that are completely acceptable among the bulk of Christians.) Unfortunately, most believers believe divorce is something that ranks among the worst sins a Christian can commit. As a result, people who are divorced or divorced and remarried are viewed as less spiritual, of less spiritual rank, somehow not up to par with the rest of the believers who are not divorced.

I'm about to throw a bombshell into the middle of all that type of thinking, so put on your seatbelt, because what I'm about to say may rock your theology and your perfect world.

Scripturally, divorce is not a sin. Yeah, that's not a typo -- *God does not see divorce as a sin.*

All of our attitudes, beliefs, and traditions that go along with divorce being one of the worst sins a person can commit – they are all in error. They're wrong.

You may be thinking: *How can you say that? Everyone knows divorce is a sin.* Well, let's take another look at it.

One reason I know divorce can't be a sin is because: God is divorced.

Yeah, that's not a typo either. *God is divorced.* So if divorce is a sin, then God is a sinner. Scripture says that God can't even be tempted with evil or sin (James 1:13).

So here is where 2 + 2 = 4. If God is divorced, yet God cannot sin, then divorce can't be a sin.

God divorced Israel. Here is the scripture that states that God is divorced:

Jeremiah 3:8 (NIV)
I gave faithless Israel her certificate of divorce and sent her away because of all her adulteries.

This scripture tells us a number of things. I'll mention 2 of them:

1.) It was better for God to divorce Israel in this situation than remain married. If it wasn't necessary, God would not have done it. So, there are situations where it's better to get divorced. What we need to find is what the Bible has to say about when divorce is permissible and even the better choice.

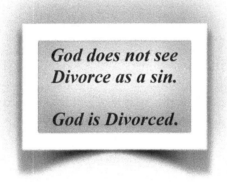

God does not see Divorce as a sin.

God is Divorced.

2.) Giving a "certificate of divorce" (legal paperwork of divorce) is not the big sin it's been made out to be, because God did it, and God cannot sin.

I realize those statements may rock your theological world, so I encourage you to stay with me and try to keep an open and objective mind to what the Bible really says about this subject. But this much is also true, even in the best-case scenario: divorce is messy, ugly, and should be avoided if at all possible. The problem is that in some cases it's not possible to avoid. Why? Because of the hearts of the people involved (we'll talk more about that later).

It was never intended by God that humans should be involved in divorce (including his own with Israel). His design -- and His designs are always best -- was that a man and woman be married and never separate. I whole-heartedly agree with and support that position.

However, because of sin, we live in a world that does not always agree with what God says is best. As a result, we have divorce. Very naturally following divorce is the issue of remarriage. Many people do not want to live alone. As Jesus and Paul said, not everyone has the gift to live alone (Matthew 19:10-12; 1 Corinthians 7:7-9). Since they don't want to simply move in with and live with someone (referred to in Hebrews 13:4 above), the issue of remarriage is often the next issue that surfaces.

We are going to look at these subjects from a very scriptural viewpoint. This book will approach divorce from a different angle than you have probably seen before. Follow the material. Think it through. Ask the Holy Spirit to help you see truth, and then decide for yourself.

What is a Covenant

Chapter 2

To establish a good understanding of how God views divorce, we will first need to understand how God views marriage. From God's perspective, marriage is a covenant, and understanding covenant is essential to understanding marriage.

Malachi 2:14 (KJV - underline added)
....yet is she thy companion, and <u>the wife of thy covenant.</u>

Malachi 2:14 (NIV - underline added)
....she is your partner, <u>the wife of your marriage covenant.</u>

Malachi 2:14 (AMP - underline added)
....yet she is your companion and <u>the wife of your covenant</u> [made by your marriage vows].

To the Western mind, covenant is a mystery. We don't understand what it is, how it functions, its purpose, why God chose it as the basic method of coming into agreement with the human race, and on the list can go. In the Western world, we basically have no clue what a covenant is. We are very familiar with contracts, but very unfamiliar with covenants. As we will see later, covenants and contracts are almost diametrically opposed.

In his dealings with the human race, God operates through covenant. Covenants began in the Garden of Eden and continue on today. In fact, everything that God does with man is by way of a covenant. It is the avenue through which God relates to the human race. There have been many blood covenants initiated by God throughout history: Adam's covenant, Noah's covenant, Abrahams's covenant, the covenant of Moses, and the new covenant that Jesus made. It's through these kinds of covenants that God relates with and interacts with the human race.

As we've already seen, from God's perspective marriage is also a covenant. In the Western world, we tend to view marriage as a contract between individuals -- not a covenant. That's why we don't understand how God views marriage. Marriage is absolutely a covenant between a man and woman. So when a marriage is dissolved, what is actually taking place is the dissolution of a covenant. That is totally different then getting out of, breaking, or dissolving a contract.

So here is the logical place to begin: we need to establish a basic understanding of covenant before we can understand God's viewpoint on divorce.

In the same way every person can enter into a blood covenant relationship with God through salvation, that same type of blood covenant relationship is pictured in marriage. In fact, the relationship between mankind and God is to be represented on this earth and pictured to the human race through the marriage covenant (Ephesians 5:22-33).

Since a marriage is a covenant and not a contract, it must be handled with covenant thinking if it is going to develop and flourish. As soon as it is thought of as a contract, it begins to go dysfunctional. It can't function under contract mentality because it's not a contract -- it's a covenant. To think covenant, we must first understand what covenant is. Then we have something with which to align our thinking.

Covenant is a huge subject. Everything in the Bible is built upon it and revolves around it. It is a subject that is way too big to fully explain in this book. Yet, I need to give an outline of what it's all about and how it works so that we can look at marriage through it, because that's how God created marriage to function and be viewed -- as a covenant. Once we have a basic understanding of the covenant of marriage, then we will be able to understand how God looks at the breaking of that covenant -- or what we normally refer to as divorce.

Covenant is found throughout the Bible. The briefest way for me to describe it is to give the steps used in making a covenant and then follow the steps with some explanation. Listed below are the steps that were used in Biblical times to make a covenant. These steps can be found in various sources where someone of eastern origin -- who knows of the process of making a traditional covenant -- explains how it is made and what it's about.

Unfortunately, there is no single place in scripture where you can find these steps laid out in order. Bits and pieces of it are seen in various places throughout the scripture. For that reason, I added some references to steps that are given. I think the reason it is not laid out in a step-by-step way in the Bible is because to the eastern mindset, how to make and live in a covenant was very well understood. They didn't need it explained to them. The Jewish people knew very well the steps needed to make covenant. If you study Eastern culture, you will very quickly find these steps. That is also true among the Native American Indians. They knew what covenant was all about and how to make it. For centuries, civilizations around the world have lived by it. In some parts of the world, they still do.

However, in the Western world, we have been trained to be *contract* orientated. We don't understand covenant. So, let's begin describing covenant by looking at the steps involved in making one. Then in the next chapter, we'll apply each of the steps to marriage. As we go through each step, keep in mind that covenant is often referred to as the "Great Exchange". That's because covenant is built on people exchanging with each other. Watch the exchanges that take place in every step of making Covenant.

Step #1: The two people making a covenant *always knew each other very well.*

    a. Noah (Genesis 6-9) -- God and Noah had a long relationship before covenant was established in chapter 9.

    b. Abraham (Genesis 12-15) -- God and Abraham went through quite a long process before covenant was actually established in chapter 15.

    c. David and Jonathan (1 Samuel 20:8,17) -- The trust and love that had grown between the two shows a long-standing relationship.

    d. The greatest covenant (Matthew 26:27-29; 1 Corinthians 11:23-26) -- The New Covenant (New Testament) that governs how God deals with man in this dispensation. The inception of this New Covenant was actually made, not between Abraham and God, but between The Father God and the Son, Jesus -- the future God-Man (Genesis 15:12-21). Then Jesus came to this earth as a man, and cut the covenant as a man -- for mankind.

One of the basic reasons for needing to *know each other very well* is that in covenant (esp. a blood covenant), you are giving your rights away (we will be seeing this in the following steps). The basic motive in making a covenant is this: I am giving myself fully to the other person for their good, not mine. I no longer am a single entity. I am no longer a single person.

Life will no longer revolve around me and what I want, need, like, plan, or desire. Life now includes another person that scripturally speaking, for

> *In the Western world, we have been trained to be Contract orientated. We don't understand Covenant.*

whom I am going to lay down my life (Gr. - 'Psuche') and serve. I am about to invest my past, present, and future into another person. I am placing all of my goals and ambitions in second place in priority to be of service to them. I am choosing to invest who I am into the other person for their benefit -- not mine. Those attitudes and mindsets are some of the basic foundation stones for making a marriage covenant.

For this reason, we need to *know this person very well* before we get into a covenant with them. To the best of our ability we need to know with *whom* we're getting into this covenant and what kind of person they are because we are giving our life to them with the focus of benefitting them.

Let me make a statement right here: covenants have different rank, authority, and order. Our covenant with God supersedes any other covenant that can be established. I say that here so that no one gets confused and thinks that a marriage covenant takes precedence over our covenant with Almighty God. God always comes first! If that order becomes confused, whatever we are giving more priority to than God, literally becomes an idol in our life. Our relationship with God always carries the highest priority in our life.

Step #2: In Biblical times, these two people would then meet in a public area like a field or courtyard. The purpose was so that *the covenant would not be a private/secret matter.* It usually included *a group of witnesses.*

    a. Noah (Genesis 9)
    b. David & Jonathan (1 Samuel 20:11,16,42)
    c. Jesus & the Father (Luke 23:25-43)
    d. People (us) joining into that Covenant (Matthew 10:32-33)

In ancient times, covenant carried tremendous power. It literally touched every area of life. It was considered a very holy thing to establish, because it would change your life forever. Alliances, partnerships, friendships, verbal and written agreements -- most everything they did in life would now be affected by the covenant that was just made. This was something that needed to be made known to the public, because it affected public life in virtually every conceivable way.

This is also true of marriage. Every relationship, friendship, partnership, agreement, and legal document will be affected by the marriage. This is one aspect of a marriage covenant that our government has built into our laws. A marriage covenant affects everything -- legally speaking. This is not true about contracts. I can enter into a contract with many different people, companies, etc., and those contracts do not affect every area of my life. Typically they only affect the realm that the contract applies to.

In ancient times, it was a privilege and honor to be a witness to a covenant being made. Witnessing a covenant being made also carried a heavy responsibility. The people who were part of this covenant making ceremony were public witnesses to the fact that everything concerning the two individuals making this covenant would now be different.

From that moment on, every person who came into the lives of the individuals who had made covenant would be affected in some way by it.

This was a time of rejoicing as well as a new beginning of great power and potential. It needed to be done in a public fashion so that it would be known to the general public.

Step #3:   The third step of cutting covenant was the exchanging of robes. This signified an *identity exchange.* They were no longer their own person. They had given away their individual identity and taken on a new identity. The individual they once were was now given away to the other, and a new identity would emerge.

   a. We are given a robe of righteousness through the covenant that Jesus cut for us. (Isaiah 6:1, 61:10; Revelation 3:18)
   b. Jesus took on our sins, and we took on His righteousness. (Romans 3:21 - 4:25)
   c. We are in Christ and He is in us. (John 15; Ephesians 1)
   d. Jesus became like us (John 1:14; Romans 8:3; 1 John 4:2), and now we are to become like Him so that when someone looks at us, they see Jesus in us. (Romans 8:29; 2 Corinthians 3:18; Philippians 3:21; 1 John 3:2)

This step carries huge implications and commands. The picture of exchanging robes is that I am "taking on" the other person and they are "taking me on" -- in the same way I would put on a coat or robe. The person I am, I willfully give away to the other. I can no longer be who I was. I now take on that other person, and they will do the same to me. We are becoming one. My identity now lies on them and theirs on me. Whatever they are, I have now agreed to take on and become whatever I can do to serve them to make them a better person. If they are poor or rich, I take that on. If they are lazy or ambitious, I take that on.

31

If they are honest or dishonest, I take that on. If they are healthy or sick, I take that on. If they are successful or unsuccessful, or whatever other of the many terms that can be used to describe a person, *I take that on for the purpose of investing myself into them for the betterment of them and their life*, and vice versa.

From my perspective, I have now committed myself to support their dreams, goals, aspirations, desires, plans, needs, wants, loves, hates, etc. -- and work with them on these things like they were my own. I choose to handle them as if I were handling myself. The person I used to be now ceases to exist, nor do I have any individual rights that stand apart from the covenant. *Following my service of God and the covenant I have with Him*, the predominant focus I now have is to serve my human covenant partner.

Now we're starting to see the importance of knowing the other person very well. This can turn into a very negative, destructive relationship; or this can be one of the best things that could have ever happened to me. This new relationship can empower both of us beyond our wildest imaginations, or it can literally become a ball-and-chain around our lives.

> *I am choosing to invest who I am into the other person for their benefit -- not mine.*

That's why it was always wise for people entering into a covenant relationship to find someone: (1.) Into whom they genuinely wanted to invest their lives; (2.) who genuinely had something to offer in return -- and the willingness to offer it -- so that the other person would help them with their own personal weaknesses; and (3.) who has realized that the focus of this relationship is built on the "gift" principle. Each partner is giving himself as a "gift" to the other person. The mindset is not about *getting* from the other person, but it has to be about *giving* to them.

Step #4: Next, they would exchange what was called the "girdle" or the "belt". This was used in ancient times to carry their weapons. This signified an *exchange of strengths.*

    a. God gave a child to Abraham when Sarah couldn't conceive. (Genesis 17)

    b. Abraham taught his household to put God first. (Genesis 18:19)
       Abraham gave Isaac back. (Genesis 22)

    c. Jesus gave Himself and His strengths to us. (2 Corinthians 12:9-10; Ephesians 6:10; Philippians 4:13)

    d. We are to give ourselves to Jesus. (Romans 12:1; 2 Timothy 2:21)

    e. Submission, obedience, and resistance of the devil and his kingdom are some strengths we give to God. (Romans 6:13; James 4:7-11; 1 Peter 5:1-10)

Covenant was created with this mindset. What are my strengths? What are their strengths? When these are mingled and made one, will this be a profitable/beneficial thing for both? This is one of the great reasons for covenant. Two working together as one can do so much more than one alone (Ecclesiastes 4:12; Matthew 18:19-20).

There is no human being alive that has all the gifts, talents, abilities, and strengths in and of themselves. God didn't design the human race to function that way (I Corinthians 12). Everybody has something to offer, and without them, the rest of us are lacking. In covenant, it's the strengths that are brought to the relationship that will produce the most good. The strengths give the empowerment.

Here is where the contract mentality of the Western world can cause problems. We are cultured to think in terms of contracts, which by nature are very selfish at their core. Let me explain: when we look at the strengths of our potential covenant partner from a contract perspective, we tend to look at how they can be of service to us and help us.

Covenant thinking looks at the strengths from a different perspective. It views the relationship predominantly from the perspective of what I can *give* to the other person, not what I can *get* from them. So, applying that to the *exchange of strengths*, we should be viewing this predominantly from the perspective of how my strengths will empower and help the other person.

Remember: I am investing my life into the other person -- that is foundational. Once I view this relationship predominantly from how they can better me and my life, I am out of covenant thinking and have gone back into contract thinking. Again I remind you: contract thinking does not function well in a marriage. It will cause a lot of problems.

I would presume by now you are seeing where this thing can become very dysfunctional. If both people entering this covenant don't carry the same understanding, expectations, beliefs, and priorities toward making this relationship work like a covenant, someone is going to be severely hurt and taken advantage of. For a covenant to work, the approach and mentality of the partners must be mutual. If one partner is trying to invest their life into the other person – but the other is not reciprocating and doing the same in return -- this relationship will become very out-of-balance. Very quickly, one person will become the abuser, and the other person will become the victim. <u>That is not what God intended.</u>

Again we see the need for Step #1 - both people need to know what the other is <u>really like</u> before they marry. If the other person doesn't understand covenant -- or are not trustworthy to carry out their end of the covenant relationship with integrity -- the marriage will either be a disaster or will very likely go through some difficult times as one or both of the partners grow and mature.

> *We are cultured in thinking in terms of contracts, which by nature are very selfish at their core.*

Step #5: The weapons were then exchanged, signifying *a common unity against the enemies of either party.* It also signified that *the two were becoming one in purpose for life.*

    a. The armor of God is given to us. (Ephesians 6:10-18)
    b. Weapons we can use that are acceptable to God.
       (Matthew 16:17-19, 18:18-20; Romans 12:17-21;
       2 Corinthians 10:4-6)
    c. A Kingdom divided against itself cannot stand.
       (Matthew 12:22-37)
    d. Becoming one in purpose. (Romans 8 - Esp. v. 28; Galatians
       5:13-26)
    e. The weapon God gave to us -- His word -- is actually
       wielded through us by the Holy Spirit.
       (Ephesians 6:17 - AMP)

Obviously, this is a further joining and becoming one. Here the focus is on becoming united against any enemies of either person. Here's where the old saying applies: "Your enemies are my enemies, and my enemies are your enemies."

We need to always remember that one of the main underlying foundations for making covenant with someone is to shore up each others' weaknesses. If possible, it's always best to make covenant with someone who is stronger in areas than we are. That way -- through covenant relationships -- we should have numerous of our weaknesses taken care of by way of our covenant partner.

This is why in a marriage covenant, the main focus needs to stay on the strengths of the other partner. Even though initially we are attracted to the other person's strengths, sadly too often we turn our focus to their weaknesses. This causes a myriad of problems in the relationship. They can usually be summarized this way: we no longer defend our covenant partner from attack; instead we often blame them for the attack or even enter into the attack against them. This all comes from focusing too much on the other person's weaknesses. Where they are weak, we are supposed to be strong for them; but too often we wound and even kill them where they are weak, rather than giving them strength.

When we take this picture and apply it to our covenant with God, it really shows what is so incredible about having a covenant with God. He has no weaknesses -- just strengths. We, on the other hand, have mostly weaknesses, and very little strength to offer Him. The thought that He would be willing to make covenant with us, when we have so little to offer Him in return, is simply mind-boggling. It's really a good picture of investing our life into someone else for their benefit and not for what can be gotten in return.

Yet there is one very huge strength we have that God needs: we live in this physical realm and have the ability to take the gospel to a lost and dying humanity. He needs that of us, and on the basis of us being willing to make that one simple exchange with Him, He is willing to give us everything that is His --blessing us beyond our wildest dreams -- in order to have access through us to a lost humanity.

> *This is why in a marriage covenant, the main focus needs to stay on the strengths of the other partner.*

That's covenant, but it's also a demonstration of God's love. He loves us and everyone in the world so completely that He is willing to do whatever He can to save all of us. The key to His plan is that He needs covenant partners who will be obedient and do what He needs done as the first reason and purpose they live. We are to lay our life down so His will can be accomplished, which is the salvation of the human race. When we take on that covenant partnership with Him, then what Jesus said in Matthew 6:25-34 takes on a whole new meaning. As our covenant partner, He will supply everything we need.

In covenant with God, His enemies are to become our enemies and our enemies are to become his enemies. As Christians, we typically like the idea of having God on our team. He takes on our enemies and helps us defeat them. However, the flip side of that coin is also to be true. We are to be on God's team and take on and defeat His enemies. The greatest challenge for us as Christians in this regard would be sin, the works of the flesh, the demonic influence, and this world's system.

A short, concise definition of that is we need to "love what God loves, and hate what God hates". To truly live in covenant with God, sin and the demonic are enemies that we need to deal with. That's why we've been asked to get their influence out of our lives (Romans 6-8; Galatians 5:13-26; Ephesians 4-6; Titus 2:11-12; James 4:4-8).

Just understanding this one step in covenant should bring new insight to the scripture:

James 4:4-5 (AMP)
[4] You [are like] unfaithful wives [having illicit love affairs with the world and breaking your marriage vow to God]! Do you not know that being the world's friend is being God's enemy? So whoever chooses to be a friend of the world takes his stand as an enemy of God. [5] Or do you suppose that the Scripture is speaking to no purpose that says, The Spirit Whom He has caused to dwell in us yearns over us and He yearns for the Spirit [to be welcome] with a jealous love?

That's covenant talk. That statement is saying that we are to take on God's enemies as our own -- not be in bed with them. When we cozy up to something that is actually an enemy of God, He views it as us committing spiritual adultery in our relationship with Him. That's heavy! It might be worth our time to research who and what God considers His enemies.

Remember: covenant is the great exchange. Jesus exchanged His righteousness for our sin, and we exchanged our sin for His righteousness (Romans 3-5).

So, to tie the great exchange principle into Step #5: to truly live in covenant with God, we need to be continually working on defeating His enemies in our lives and with those on whom we have influence.

Step #6: The next step in the process was to kill an animal and split it in half. The pieces were arranged so that the two people who were making covenant could walk around and between the pieces in a figure 8 fashion. This was called the walk of death. It signified that *each person was dying to what they used to be: their desires, goals, ambitions, and anything else that would ever cause any type of conflict between them, or hinder them from walking in complete harmony and becoming one.* Then, each one would point at the pieces and declare that this is what God should do to them (as was done to the pieces) if they were to ever break the covenant.

    a. Abraham's Covenant (Genesis 15:9-10)
    b. David and Jonathan (1 Samuel 20:3-4,14-15)
    c. Jesus and us. In this covenant, Jesus was the sacrifice. (Mark 10:45; Luke 9:23-24; John 10:15, 17; Romans 5:8, ch. 6 & 8; 2 Corinthians 4:7-12; Galatians 2:20)

This signified that each person involved in making this covenant was going to die to who and what they were for the purpose of becoming one with each other in covenant. Anything that would hinder that uniting process from taking place needed to be put out of their lives and put to death.

When this is applied to our entering into the New Testament covenant with the Father God, anything that separates the human being from God must be removed from our lives, or as the picture shows, we must die to it. In covenant with God, we need to die to the old nature of sin that lives in our flesh.

Our life is really not our own. We have been bought with a price. That's why we are to honor God with our spirit and with everything that happens while we're on this earth in this fleshly body (I Corinthians 6:20). As it says in Luke 9:23-24 and Galatians 2:20, we are to be dead to our life, and Jesus is to be living through us just as Jesus died so we could have life through him.

As believers, we are in a position of being blessed by God (Ephesians 1:3). We have been redeemed from the curse of the law so that the blessing might be ours (Galatians 3:13-14), and just like everything else that God has given to us, we need to learn to live by faith and be obedient in what has been given to us. The curse and death for disobedience are still very much alive (Romans 6:23; 8:12-13). Disobedience (or sin) will open our lives to the reestablishment of the curse in our lives. God watches over the blessing and the curse to make sure His word is fulfilled (Deuteronomy 27-30).

I know that's Old Testament, and some feel it does not have an affect in believers' lives in our dispensation. However, when the Apostle Paul talks about sin being able to bring death into our lives (Romans 6-8), he's referring to the same thing the Old Testament was referring to in the word "curse". The curse came because of sin, and it brought death. That scenario will still establish in a persons life if we persist on living in sin (this theme is found throughout the New Testament, especially in the books the Apostle Paul wrote). If Christian believers persist in living in sin, it will produce death in their lives. In the same way, living

> *Anything that would hinder that uniting process from taking place needed to be put out of their lives and put to death.*

by the Holy Spirit and obedience goes hand in hand with blessing (Romans 6:1-2, 11-16, 20-23; 8:1-4, 9-13. Remember: this was written to believers, not unbelievers.).

We are free of the curse because of grace. And yet, even grace tells us to say NO to sin (Titus 2:11-12).

Concerning marriage, here's what Step #6 is about: it pictures each party dying to whatever would cause problems or conflict between them so they can live in complete harmony with each other. When our life is too much about us -- and not our covenant partner -- disunity and dissension begin to develop. They are the seeds that will eventually cause a person to make choices and decisions that don't have the best interests of their partner in mind. They may even exclude how the choices and decisions will affect their partner in favor of themselves, someone, or something else. As we will see when we make the deeper applications of covenant to marriage, once that happens, we are beginning to cross over into the realm that could break the covenant.

Step #7: Next, while standing between the pieces, each person would cut their wrist or hand, and these would be joined in a symbol of mingling the blood with each other. This was the heart of establishing or cutting a blood covenant, and it *symbolized becoming one.*

  a. The blood used in Noah's covenant (Genesis 9)
  b. The blood used in Abrahams' covenant (Genesis 15)
  c. The blood used in Moses' covenant (Exodus 24)
  d. The blood in Jesus' covenant (Matthew 26:26-29; Romans 3:21-4:12; 1 Corinthians 11:23-26; 2 Corinthians 4:7-12)

Covenant is all about *becoming one.* It is shown over and over and over again in the Bible.

41

Scripture says the life is in the blood (Leviticus 17:11). This step in establishing covenant was to show that the people making the covenant were joining with each other down to their very life source -- their blood.

This is the step we usually see in old Western movies when a Native American would make covenant with a cowboy. They would cut their hands and mingle their blood together. That concept came from this step of making covenant. Even in the old movies, it depicted that from that time forward, the two would do everything in their power to take care of and protect the other person.

I realize that when couples become married, they don't cut their wrists or hands and mingle the blood. But as we will see later, there is a blood element that takes place in marriage.

> *Covenant is all about becoming one.*
>
> *It is shown over and over again in the Bible.*

Step #8: Ground/mud (sometimes gunpowder) would be placed into the cut. This would cause a very definite scar. This was *a lasting sign of the covenant, and an outward evidence that the person with the scar was in covenant with someone.*

    a. Noah's covenant and the rainbow (Genesis 9)
    b. Abraham's covenant and circumcision (Genesis 17:9-14)

    c. Moses' covenant as an extension of Abraham's covenant
       (Leviticus 12:1-3 -- Circumcision)
    d. Jesus' covenant and the circumcision of the heart & love
       (Romans 2:28-29; John 13:34-35)

Let's look back to the Native American tradition. From what I've found in my research, one of the reasons they would greet others with the uplifted open hand was so that those they were greeting would know they were in covenant with someone else. The scar in the palm of their hand -- that was left from making covenant with someone -- would be visible to the person they were greeting.

This was very important in those times where there was no official law or justice system. Society had to have it's own methods of self-protection and self-preservation. One way was to be in covenant with another person. Then, if an enemy was thinking of harming one person, they would see the *visible sign or token* of covenant on the hand (the scar) and know they were in covenant with someone else. Often, they wouldn't know who that other person was, which increased the effectiveness of the scar. All they knew was that if they caused harm to or killed this person or their family, a different person would come after them. In doing one harm, they would have just made an enemy with the other because of that covenant. It was a great deterrent from someone randomly trying to do some evil or damaging thing to people who were in covenant.

If someone had multiple scars on either or both hands, it was that much more of a deterrent. They were in covenant with multiple people. So when you were taking on one person, in actuality you were taking on many people, families, or tribes.

The "scar" of covenant in the New Testament for Christians is love (John 13:34-35). When we handle people and situations in a loving manner, we are showing we are in covenant with God. Because of the *exchange of enemies* that takes place in covenant (Step #5), should someone deal with us in an immoral or unrighteous manner, they will quickly find themselves dealing with God who now stands opposed to them. Because we are in covenant with Him, our enemies are His enemies, and He will fight for the one who is in covenant with Him.

Step #9: At this point, *blessings would be spoken* as a result of fulfilling the covenant. *Curses were also spoken,* which would take affect if the covenant was ever broken.

 a. Noah (Genesis 9:8-17)
 b. Abraham (Genesis 17)
 c. Moses (Deuteronomy 28 & 30)
 d. Jesus (Galatians 3. - Esp v. 13-14; Hebrews 10 - Esp. v. 19-39)

The curse of the Old Testament law, or for sinning, is still very much active (Romans 6:23; 8:12-13). In Galatians 3:10-14, we are told that Jesus came and made a new covenant, which redeemed us from the curse of the Old Testament law. If we -- by faith -- will align ourselves with the new covenant of grace that Jesus established, we can live free from the curses that come as a result of breaking the law or sinning. In that case, the only thing that remains for us is the blessing. That should obviously be our goal.

When God established the covenant with Abraham, it is very obvious from scripture that blessings and curses were spoken (Genesis 15, 17; and Deuteronomy 27-30 which was an addition to Abraham's covenant until Jesus came). When Jesus came, He died for all the curses that were to rest on people because of their sins. Jesus took that curse for us (Galatians 3:10-14). All that remains for believers are the blessings that were spoken in Abraham's covenant. So, if someone says the curses from Abraham's or Moses' covenants no longer apply, then the blessings from those covenants can no longer apply either. Both the blessings and the curses are still active. The only way we can get free from the curses of the law is to join ourselves with Jesus' covenant. He took the curse of our sin, so it would not rest or settle on us.

The two main commands of Jesus' covenant are these: (1.) to love God with all our heart, soul, mind, and strength; and (2.) to love our neighbor as ourselves (Mark 12:29-31). When we apply the first command to everyday life, we find the Bible saying over and over that -- if we love God -- we will obey Him (John 14:15, 21, 23, 24, 31; 15:9-17; 1 John 5:2-3; 2 John 6). This is not only the sign of covenant, it is also the requirement to remain in covenant. Our total commitment in love to God and our fellow human beings is absolutely vital to remaining untouched by the curse and living only in blessing.

When two people are born-again or saved from their sins as the New Testament declares, they are free from the curse of the law. Since they are free from the curse, their marriage should also be free from any curse. That's one of the reasons the Bible says in 2 Corinthians 6:14-17 (KJV & AMP) that a believer should not be unequally yoked with (or "married to" when applying it to this book) someone who is an unbeliever. When that is done, according to those verses, we are trying to join two opposite kingdoms (the Kingdom of God and of the devil). This is not going to work well, because you are taking someone who is still subject to the curse and trying to unite them with someone who is free from the curse and should be living in only blessing. God says: don't do that. Why would He say that? One reason is that such a union will allow the curses of the unsaved partner to infiltrate the entire marriage covenant. Here again we see principles of covenant being shown in the scripture.

Step #10: The two people involved in making the covenant would exchange names. This again signified *the exchange of identities and becoming one.*

    a. Genesis 17:5 -- Abram was changed to Abr-*ah*-am. God took part of His name Y-ah-weh and put it into Abram's name.

    b. Genesis 17:15 -- Sarai was changed to Sar-*ah*, again taking part of God's name, and putting it into her name.

    c. Genesis 24:12, 27, 42, 48 (and throughout the Old Testament) -- God became known by the name of *"The God of Abraham."*

    d. Acts 11:26 - The followers of Jesus are known as *Christians,* taking the name *Christ* and making it into a new name by which we are called.

    e. Matthew 8:20 - Jesus became known as the *"Son of Man,"* again taking the human name *Man* and putting it into a name that refers to Jesus.

> *It is saying that they are no longer the person they used to be, but now have become a new person with a new identity.*

In the exchange of names, we are seeing again that the pre-covenant person no longer exists. This is re-emphasized by each person taking on a new name. That new name identifies them with their new covenant partner. It is saying that they are no longer the person they used to be, but now have become a new person with a new identity. The reason they are a new person is due to the fact that they have joined their lives in service to another.

An example of that in the Old Testament is Abraham and Sarah. Before they were in covenant with God, they were known as Abram and Sarai (Genesis 16:1). When they were brought into covenant with God, they had a name change. Here's how that worked:

One of God's primary names is "Y<u>ah</u>weh."

God took the "ah" part of His name and gave it to Abram and Sarai. The result was that their names were now Abr<u>ah</u>am and Sar<u>ah</u> (Genesis 17:5, 15).

Also God took on Abraham's name by being called "The God of Abraham" (Genesis 26:24, 28:13).

In ancient covenants, both partners exchanged parts of their names. This confirmed a true, equal identity exchange. In the Western culture, most of the time it's the bride who takes on the groom's last name. To be consistent with a true covenant exchange, both partners should take on some portion of each other's name.

Step #11: The two people involved in the covenant ate a covenant meal. This signified that each person was *taking the other into their very being or life -- becoming one.*

    a. Abraham (Genesis 18)
    b. Moses (Exodus 24:11)
    c. Jesus (Matthew 26:26-29; 1 Corinthians 11:23-26)
    d. The future marriage supper in heaven (Revelation 19:1-9; specifically v. 9)

The physical act of eating with your new covenant partner was very significant. This was done by the individuals feeding each other. They would eat the same food or eat from the same bowl. In some cases, they would literally take the food in their hands and put it into the other person's mouth.

This showed that the two people were becoming one. But it also went much deeper than that by showing that they were willing to take the things they need to sustain their own lives and give them to the other to sustain his life. A vivid picture of this is how Jesus will serve His people at the Marriage Supper. In Luke 12:35-37, Jesus drew the picture that He would serve the food to us at the meal which culminates our covenant with Him. That is so awesome!

When this step is applied to receiving the Lord's Supper, Communion or the Eucharist, it becomes very powerful. Every time we receive communion, we are saying that anything and everything we need to sustain life has been provided by our God through Jesus Christ. It also speaks to our proclaiming and identifying with Jesus' death (1 Corinthians 11:26). When we proclaim the Lord's death in the symbols of the Lord's Supper, we are also proclaiming our own death to sin and our old nature. In our death to what we were, we are able to take on the new life that Jesus has purchased for us (Romans 6; Galatians 2:20, 5:13-25; Ephesians 4:7-5:21; Colossians 2:6-3:17). This ongoing process of sanctification, dying to our old self, and taking on the new self that is made to be like Christ is a daily process. It is pictured in the covenant meal.

Step #12: From that point on they were known as *friends*. That term signified that a blood covenant relationship had been formed.

    a. Abraham (Isaiah 41:8; James 2:23)
    b. Moses (Exodus 33:11)
    c. Jesus (John 15:13-15)

The term "friend" is used very loosely in Western civilization compared to how it was used in covenant. In the ancient eastern civilization, when a person referred to someone as their friend, they were stating they were in covenant with that person. In their lifetime they would become friends with a very small, selective, particular group of people. They may only have made friends (or covenant) with one person over their entire lifetime. To be a person's friend in covenant was a position that was taken very seriously, but also carried a great deal of power.

Remember, I said that covenant is often referred to as the "great exchange". Did you see how in making a covenant with someone, we intentionally exchange every facet and aspect of our life with another person? We take on their life and become one with them, and they take on our life and become one with us. The underlying purpose for the whole thing is to invest our life into another. We will do everything we can to serve each other in whatever ways are necessary to prosper each other in every area of their life. Ideally, we will look for someone who can bring strengths to our life where we are weak, and they will look for the same in us. In God's case, He has no weaknesses like we do, but He does have a need.

When we are looking at covenant, weaknesses can also be referred to as "needs". Each party has a need. The overall goal is to have a relationship that is made stronger by both parties strengths and fulfilling what is lacking in the other person's weakness, or in God's case -- a need.

What was God's need? He needed to get back into rulership of the human race so He could save it from eternal destruction. Adam and Eve had given that rulership position to Satan when they chose to disobey God and obey Satan. To keep man from being eternally destroyed by their new master, God needed to get back into the human race in a way where He could exercise His authority and change the mess Adam and Eve had just created for the human race.

That's why He needed blood covenant. It is the highest form of covenant that can be made. It allows a pure exchange of the entire life and identity of one person with another. He did this in a few very calculated and intentional covenants. The first one was the covenant with Noah. In this covenant God preserved the human race from destroying itself through sin and interbreeding with fallen angels. This covenant helped the human race to stay alive long enough for God to turn things around.

God needed direct access into the human race. He found this access through the covenant He made with Abraham and the exchange of "sons". God asked Abraham to sacrifice his son for God, which gave God the right to now exchange and sacrifice His son (Jesus) for the human race. Abraham's covenant was crucial to the salvation of the human race. Once that access was given, God was now in the process of setting everything up to give His son as the ultimate sacrifice for our sin.

> *Blood Covenant is the Highest form of Covenant that can be made.*

But again, man was bent on self-destruction. So God established another covenant with Moses to keep His people on track until the Savior would come to this earth. The covenant of Moses, or what we generally refer to as the Old Testament law, was not part of God's original intent. He wanted to go from Abraham's covenant directly to the new covenant that Jesus made. But Abraham's lineage was in the process of destroying itself through sin. They would not have lasted long enough for Jesus to come to this earth and establish the new covenant and be our savior. That's one of the basic reasons why the Bible says the law was "added". It was added because of transgression or sin (Galatians 3:19). It was added to Abraham's covenant with God for a specific duration of time -- until Jesus came.

The focus of Abraham's covenant was Jesus (the *seed* - Galatians 3:19). That *seed* was the person to whom God referred in Genesis 3:15 when He told Eve that her *seed* would crush Satan's head. That *seed* is Jesus. He is the focal point of the entire human race. From the time of Adam and Eve's sin, to the new heaven and new earth which is still coming in our future, Jesus and the covenant He established to save the human race is the epicenter of our entire existence. Jesus died, gave His blood on the cross, and exchanged His life for ours, creating the last covenant that God would ever need to be able to help the human race. Through that blood covenant, Jesus exchanged His life for ours. And the only thing we need to do to become part of that exchange is ask Jesus to forgive our sins and put our trust in Him for our salvation. That opens the door to the whole thing.

God needed rightful and legitimate access to the human race to be able to establish Jesus' covenant. That rightful access came through the covenant He made with Abraham.

Everything God does on this earth with the human race is always centered in a covenant. That's why marriage is a blood covenant. It was one of the first things God did in His involvement with the human race through Adam and Eve (Matthew 19:4-6).

Covenant Applied to Marriage

Chapter 3

Now let's look at how the steps of covenant apply to marriage.

It's interesting, but most people don't realize that the average Christian wedding ceremony in Western culture is based on the steps required to create a covenant. Even though we don't carry out each step as they do in Eastern culture, what each step signifies is very obvious in the marriage ceremony. Let's take a look at each step and briefly apply it to the typical American Christian wedding ceremony.

Step #1: The two people making a Covenant *always knew each other very well.*

Now that we have a basic understanding of the commitment level required to establish a covenant, this step is pretty easy to understand. Before anyone should enter into a covenant relationship where they are committing themselves to do whatever is necessary to serve, bless, and prosper their covenant partner -- it would be good to *really* know the person with whom you are making this agreement. This isn't something to take lightly.

Because the average person no longer understands covenant and what it's all about, we often don't integrate this step into the decision-making process of choosing a spouse and marriage. Realistically, before we give our life away, it would be good to know what this person to whom we arc making that level of commitment is like. Yet, people are getting married all the time with basically one concept in mind -- this marriage will be built like a contract. In America, we don't think we need to know a person very well to make a contract with them, so we take that thinking into marriage. After all, if the contract doesn't work out, we'll just go to court and break the contract (divorce).

> *Realistically, before we give our life away, it would be good to know what this person is like to whom we are making that level of commitment.*

It's sad that in our culture, we are forced to make some of the biggest decisions of our entire lives when we are the least qualified to make them. Marriage is one of those decisions. I've watched people get married (I'm sure you have too) who really didn't know each other very well. They didn't take the time nor did they have the tools to know how to really be open and honest with each other. It's like the old saying goes: "You don't really know someone until you live with them". During the dating process, all that is ever seen is the "best" of who the other person is. They don't typically work the dating process long enough to really get to know them. Anyone can make a good impression for a few weeks or months, but eventually the facade breaks down, and we see what they're really like. The sad part is that by that time, people have usually married. Now what do they do? The partner is no longer the person they thought they had married. Too often, had they known what this person was really like, they wouldn't have married them.

My advice, which I believe goes along with the first step in making a covenant, is to go slowly -- give the relationship a good amount of time so you can get to *really* know them. Because, from God's perspective, what a man and a woman are about to do in making covenant is no small thing.

I think this is a good time to address what has become the solution to not knowing the person well enough before we marry: "living together" for a while. By moving in together, we get to know them. Here's the problem with that line of thinking: living together typically includes being sexually active. Some would argue that's all part of getting to know them. Well, that's true, but it's also part of being deceived; and once we're deceived, we can't see straight anymore, so the chances of really giving the relationship a fair start are almost non-existent.

Let me explain: I realize we are living in a permissive culture, and being sexually intimate before marriage is rarely viewed as a big thing anymore. However, from God's perspective *it is a big thing*. It is part of the final joining of a man and a woman. It is part of making a "blood covenant" (we'll discuss this more later). From God's perspective, having sex before the other steps of the covenant are in place is equal to taking advantage of and violating the other person. We say it's about the other person, but more often than not it's a self-satisfying act. It's not about them; it's about us. That is already a violation of Godly love and covenant. It's not going to produce any long-term good.

That's why from God's perspective, it's a sin. Yeah, I said it. Scripturally, having sex outside of an established covenant is sin. It's called sexual immorality (Galatians 5:19; Ephesians 4:17-19, 5:3; Colossians 3:5; Hebrews 13:4; Revelation 21:8, 22:15 -- All NIV), fornication

(Acts 15:20; 1 Corinthians 6:18, 7:2, 10:8; 1 Thessalonians 4:3), or adultery (1 Corinthians 6:9; 2 Peter 2:14). It's a violation of how God designed an intimate relationship between a man and a woman to be established. In some form, it will produce death in the relationship that -- if not dealt with -- will either kill the relationship entirely, or damage it so badly it will be like a wounded animal struggling to stay alive -- often taking years to recover.

Sin is deceptive.

I'm sure someone is saying to himself, "I don't see what the big deal is." Well, let me try to explain: when you make a covenant with someone -- *it is a big deal.* You are giving your life away to another person. To do that, we should know them very well before we make that decision. The problem is that sin is deceptive. Once you willfully engage with it, it will deceive you and ultimately bring death into your life (Romans 7:11; Titus 3:3; Hebrews 3:13). Scripturally, sex before marriage is a sin. Sooner or later, it will deceive you and produce death (Romans 6:23; 8:12-13).

Be sure you understand that. Sin is deceptive. The problem with deception is this: the people who are deceived rarely recognize it. That's why it's called deception. What happens is, the person -- being deceived by the sin they are in -- is not able to clearly see the other person for who they really are. The result is that they marry someone thinking they know them, only to find out after the marriage that the person is totally different than who they thought he or she was. Right from the beginning, the first step in establishing covenant never had a chance to do its work. Now there are problems and trouble in the marriage that will try to destroy the covenant. In reality, it could have been avoided if the first step of covenant would have played out and the exchange of the blood step would have waited until the end where it's intended to be.

God is not trying to take away our fun. He's trying to protect us from making a big mistake.

What if someone was involved sexually before they were married, and now their marriage is struggling? You are not doomed. That's what forgiveness is for. Go to God and ask Him for forgiveness. If you can do this as a couple -- even better. Then, get some understanding of what sex is about from God's perspective, and grow and mature into applying it and living it in your marriage. God's grace and forgiveness are two awesome and amazing gifts. They give us the ability to start over and do it correctly. And by the way, I realize this might be hard to grasp, but from God's perspective, there is no limit to how often we can be forgiven and start over. We can keep working at it until we get it right.

Step #2: In Biblical times, these two people would then meet in a public area like a field or courtyard. The purpose was so that *the covenant would not be a private/secret matter.* It usually included *a group of witnesses.*

This is why the average wedding is a very public event. Many friends, relatives, and other people we know are invited to the wedding. Covenants were designed to be made known in a very public fashion. It was part of the reason for their existence. A secret covenant did not serve the people who made the covenant as well as a public covenant. Having a good number of people at a wedding is the result of this covenant step.

However, having a large number of people attend a wedding will not make the covenant stronger. Not everyone in the world that you know has to be there. If it is done publicly, and the event is registered with the courthouse, the word will get out that you are married.

Yet, there is one thing that is important: the attendees should know they are there to witness the making of a covenant. The overall group of witnesses can be broken down into three distinct subgroups: (1.) the general public, (2.) the personal attendants, and (3.) the best man and the maid of honor. Each of them has a distinct role to play in the formation of the new covenant. But, as a general statement, it could be said that they are all in attendance to support and be a public witness to what is about to happen. Someone is getting married, or in other words, a new covenant is being made.

Those in attendance should be in support of the couple and their marriage. I've counseled and prayed with couples who have had an up-hill struggle throughout their entire marriage. When we've traced it back, often we find there were people at the forming of the covenant (wedding) who were not in agreement with them getting married. They verbally spoke against it, and cursed it from its inception. As a result, the couple seemed to struggle at every turn in their marriage. Scripturally speaking, our words are important and do carry power. We choose life and death with what we say (Deuteronomy 30:11-19). Once we prayed and separated the couple from the curses that were spoken over them, it's amazing how their life settled down and moved forward more easily.

Here are a few examples of what I've heard and seen.

There have been numerous times -- at either the wedding reception, or as people were walking in the door before the wedding had begun – that I've heard people say things such as,

"I give them six months and they'll be headed for divorce."
"These two should never be getting married - it will never work."
"This is a joke if I've ever seen one."

I've heard all kinds of goofy things being said that are actually cursing the success of the marriage. It definitely isn't blessing the couple or wishing them the best for their future together. There have been times I've felt like stopping the person and asking them, "why are you here anyway? For the free food? To have a party? Because by what you're saying, it's definitely not to support the bride and groom in what they are trying to do." My advice: if you know someone is not supportive of your marriage, don't invite them to the wedding. Making covenant is a huge spiritual event. It's best if everyone witnessing the event is in agreement for the best of the couple.

Step #3: Then the two people cutting covenant would exchange robes. This signified an *identity exchange.* They were no longer their own person. They had given away their individual identity, and taken on a new identity. The individual they once were was now given away to the other, and a new identity would emerge.

Identity exchange is a big thing in our weddings. After a wedding, it will show up in every legal document we have. Names are changed on social security cards and other governmental documents. Property ownership, filing of taxes, insurances, trusts, wills, buying and selling of property, our credit score, our reputation – they're all affected by a marriage. Legally the people who just entered into covenant are no longer single entities. They are a new entity emerging into society.

The reality of the identity exchange is very obvious in our society. Even though a bride and groom typically don't exchange robes or coats at a wedding ceremony any more, the ramifications of the identity exchange are built into just about every aspect of our society.

Covenant was designed by God to remove the two individual identities and replace them with a new one.

"Has not the Lord made them one? In flesh and spirit they are his…." (Malachi 2:15).

"Haven't you read…the two will become one flesh? So they are no longer two, but one" (Matthew 19:4-5).

Exchanging identities and becoming "one with" your spouse seems like a very difficult thing for the Western mindset to understand. Once we are "one" with our partner, we don't identify ourselves as a personal single identity. Here are some examples of how that changes our thinking, speech, and actions:

> "I have my friends, and he has his." The truth is, in covenant, if they are not both of your friends, they can't be either of your friends. Why? You are one unit, not two. What happens with one will directly affect the other. That cannot be separated, even for friends.

With the principle of what I just said above, having much of anything separate in a covenant is a signal there is an identity exchange problem. Here are some more examples:

> "I have my money, and she has hers." The truth: in true covenant, all the money, possessions, and property belongs to both of you.

> "She's not allowed to drive my car, she has her own." The truth: with that kind of thinking, the identity exchange has not fully taken place yet.

> "She's learned that my side of the closet is mine." The truth: nothing is exclusively owned or managed in covenant.

"Her relatives are the issue." The <u>truth</u>: when you made covenant, they became your relatives too.

"Those are his children, and these are my children." <u>The Truth</u>: when you made covenant, all of them became "your" children before God. He will hold both of you responsible for all of them. You are one -- not two.

"I will do whatever I want with my inheritance. It's none of his / her business. It's mine from my parents." <u>The truth</u>: in covenant there is no such thing as an exclusive "mine" concerning anything. When we make covenant, we are giving up our right to "mine". It is now "ours".

"I run the checkbook and make the money / business decisions in our marriage. It's none of her business." <u>The truth</u>: any decision one partner makes is the other's business. There isn't one thing that you can divide out and take exclusive control of. That individual identity was given away when you were joined in covenant with your spouse. There is no longer a "me" in the picture; it's all to be about "us".

"I don't really care for it. I wouldn't have bought it, but she liked it." <u>The truth</u>: when you commit to purchase something together, it's an "us" thing now. It's "ours". To separate that simply separates the relationship and covenant.

"But I never agreed to buy it. In fact, I didn't want it." <u>The truth</u>: that statement shows the covenant and oneness is either struggling, or was never fully established. In covenant, one partner doesn't do things with which the other doesn't agree. It would be like a person being double-minded or confused. In their own head, they don't agree with what they're buying for themselves, but they buy it anyway. We would say that person probably has mental issues. The same is true in covenant.

Remember -- it's two people in ONE identity. One person is not split or dual unless they have mental struggles. One person is ONE. That's what a covenant is to produce: ONE identity.

These are just a few examples of when the true "oneness" of identity has not taken hold in a marriage. The thinking, speaking, and actions readily reveal that we still consider ourselves our own individual unit. "I can do what I want." Actually, in covenant, we gave away the right to do as we please. Who did we give it to? We gave it to our covenant partner.

Step #4: Next they would exchange what was called the "girdle" or the "belt". This was used in ancient times to carry their weapons. This signified an *exchange of strengths.*

In the Western culture we no longer physically exchange a belt at a wedding. At least, I've never seen it happen.

When we marry someone, we typically look at all the good things they can bring to the relationship. We look forward to the strengths they will add to our lives and the strengths we can add to their lives. So, the concept or picture is there whether we physically exchange belts at the ceremony or not.

People usually do not enter into a marriage covenant if the only thing they can see is how badly this will turn out for them or all the weaknesses they will now have to live with because of the other person being part of their lives. They don't focus on how this person will be a negative or a detractor from their overall life.

It is obvious that the reason we make covenant with someone is to receive and give of the strengths each person brings to the relationship. I've found that in a good marriage, the person with the strengths in certain areas is the one who takes care of those areas. In a struggling marriage, activities and responsibilities are divided up by gender, cultural or religious expectations, etc.

The best marriages are made by two people who are not intimidated to exchange their strengths in the relationship.

Too often they are not divided up according to who has the ability or strength to do the job the best. That again shows our lack of understanding of how a covenant should function. That's what making covenant is all about.

For example, if one partner is better at finances, it would be in the best interest of the marriage to let that person have more jurisdiction over the finances. Just because you're the man doesn't mean you have to be the one taking care of the finances, particularly when you don't handle money very well. This is the type of thinking that can cause a lot of problems in a marriage. It's not covenant type of thinking. It's based on something else, but not covenant.

Here is another example: sometimes culture or religion dictates that the man make all the major decisions (often without any input from the wife). What a mistake. Again, it is the opposite of what covenant is all about. Too often, the man makes some kind of stupid decision, and then the wife and family have to pick up the pieces or live with it the best they can. If she had been included as an equal covenant partner, she never would have made the dumb decision. Why? Because she has more strengths in that particular area.

I say it again: realize that both of you are bringing strengths to the relationship. Guys, she is called your helpmate ("help meet" - Genesis 2:18, KJV) because God wants you to let her help. Get off your high horse of thinking you are the "gift" to this marriage and somehow God endowed you with all the ability to make every decision for the marriage and the family. She's a gift to this marriage as much as you are, and believe it or not, she has some God-given abilities also, even to the point that in some areas her abilities are stronger than yours. Wow, can it be?

Use some common sense and let her help! The same can be said for the wife. There are some things your husband is good at -- he has strengths in those areas. Move over and let him go at it. Both of you need to work through the insecurities -- or macho man / empowered woman attitudes, weird religious teaching, cultural norms, etc. -- and let the other partner flow in what they're good at. It doesn't discredit you. It will make you look better. Usually it's no secret to the people around us when we don't know what we're doing. Everybody sees it. So get over the personal issues, whatever they may be, and *exchange your strengths.*

When people become stubborn and -- because of gender, age, or whatever -- decide that they need to be in charge of a certain area whether they are good at it or not, it will cause a lot of problems in that marriage.

The best marriages are made by two people who are not intimidated to exchange their strengths in the relationship. Do the things at which best, and let the other person do the things at which they are best.

Step #5: The weapons were then exchanged, signifying *a common unity against the enemies of either party.* It also signified that *the two were becoming one in purpose for life.*

Now, that would be an interesting wedding. The best man and the maid-of-honor are packing all the weapons of the bride and groom because someplace in the ceremony they are going to exchange them. I'd be willing to go out of my way to attend a wedding where I could see that.

> *In a true covenant, one partner will lay their life down to protect the other.*

However, the concept is absolutely intact and true in a marriage. When a person marries, they are taking on any enemies the other person may have, from the IRS, to outstanding financial obligations, to bad relationships, sometimes even including the in-laws. It's amazing where enemies will surface.

I can say this with certainty: if you want to create problems and possibly destroy your marriage, just go ahead and side with your partner's enemies. That will not go well. That's another reason why it's good to know what you are getting into before you marry them. Count the cost before you go to war.

On the other hand, one of the worst things one could do is to pick on or come against a husband or wife of a good marriage. You will find there is an underlying attitude that flows through any man or woman who has committed to their marriage. They will instinctively defend the other person against whomever or whatever.

I've watched people make fun of this quality and insinuate that this is not a good thing. However, in watching marriages for many years, I find that being able to remain in unity against the attacks that come against either party, or the marriage, is one of the main contributing factors to a long and successful marriage. Once one of the individuals in the covenant feels vulnerable, abandoned, betrayed, or unsafe by their partner's choice to side with others, that marriage is headed for a lot of trouble.

The almost instinctive quality to stand by and defend one's partner that is found in the human being on the day of their wedding is a gift of God in the birthing of their covenant. It needs to remain intact through the remainder of their marriage. It is a characteristic of being in a covenant relationship. In a true covenant, one partner will lay their life down to protect the other (John 15:13). However, it is good to learn how to harness that quality of defending the other, so that it doesn't get both of you in trouble or make you look foolish.

The purpose of making the other partner's life the best it can possibly be is a very precious and important aspect of a covenant. This includes dealing with the day-to-day minor issues of people who don't like or maybe even hate one partner or the other. But it also includes the major issues of being under the threat of physical attack or death.

In covenant, both partners stay united against an enemy, and are willing to lay down their own reputation, desires, goals, friends, property, and even their physical life to protect their covenant partner. A huge aspect of desiring to be faithful to and committed to someone revolves around feeling safe with them. One of the greatest ways of making someone feel safe is to stand by their side and defend them in the face of criticism, put-downs, belittling, accusations, or whatever kind of attack may come.

But what if they are guilty? What if they were wrong in what they did. Should I lie for them? Should I cover for them and make them appear innocent, when I know they are wrong? Absolutely not! If you do that, now you are violating your greatest covenant, which is with God. We should never lie or deceive to cover for or protect our spouse. There are other ways to handle it. For instance, simply excuse yourself (or both of you) from the conversation so you can talk about it and get on the same page before you deal with the situation or other people. I have never run into an instance where the accuser was not able to wait. They usual-

> *The almost instinctive quality to stand by and defend one's partner that is found in the human being on the day of their wedding is a gift of God in the birthing of their covenant. It needs to remain intact through the remainder of their marriage.*

ly don't want to, but they can. Or, simply tell them you want to talk it over privately, and once that is done, you'll make a decision on it; or if appropriate, get back to them on what you decided. Draw the boundary for yourselves that says, "I need to talk to my wife / husband first so I can be clear on what we're talking about, and then I'll get back to you." Set the boundary that you need some time. Then keep your word. Since you initiated the boundary, you must initiate getting back to the accuser. Do not be the kind of person who avoids or tries to find a way out of dealing with the issue.

During that interval of time, a number of things are going to need to be addressed between the two of you:

1.) Find the truth about whatever the accusation or attack is about. You will not be able to handle the situation correctly until you both get on the same page with the entire truth.

2.) Reject the fallen human nature desire to lie, hide the truth, run from the situation, accuse back, or find a way to get out of dealing with the situation.

Now you will discover the depth of your own spirituality and maturity. The more ungodly and immature you are, the more you will gravitate toward responding in a way that is neither Godly nor mature. You may find some weaknesses inside of yourself or your marriage that needs some work.

Ungodliness will lie, steal, cheat, shut down and say nothing, or do whatever it has to in order to get through the situation. Godliness will be truthful, own its choices or behavior, be forthright, and do whatever is necessary to make restitution and fix the problem or situation.

Immaturity will handle a difficult situation by using the blame game. It has to be someone else's fault. Immaturity NEVER likes to admit it was wrong or be at fault. It has to be someone else's fault as to why the situation is the way it is. It can't be mine. One type of immature person will yell, scream, threaten, verbally/emotionally/physically abuse, shift the blame, cuss, swear, and basically do whatever is needed to get the other person to back off and/or win in the situation. The other common expression of immaturity is to simply refuse to talk about it. Immaturity will go silent. The flawed logic is that if I don't engage with you, there's nothing you can do about it. You can't make me talk, and in that way I still maintain control.

Many times we have to deal with these immaturities and issues within the marriage before we are able to go back to our accusers and deal with them. These times of confrontation will give us good opportunities to see who we really are and then grow and mature.

> 3.) Realize that wherever you and your spouse are not in agreement, it will surface during this time. This is not unusual, but it will have to be dealt with, and the two of you need to be in agreement before going back into whatever the situation is that needs to be resolved.

It is much better to deal with this privately than in front of others. This is another reason to stay in unity about never taking the side of an attacker or enemy. Back away and deal with your personal stuff -- privately. Then go back to the other people and deal with them and that situation with a united front.

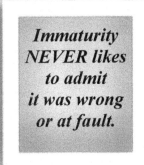

Immaturity NEVER likes to admit it was wrong or at fault.

Realize something here: in many cases, the attacker or enemy can be your own children. Don't get into a fight in front of them. Deal with your covenant partner privately, and then go back to them in unity -- no matter what age they may be (I'll say more about this later).

> 4.) If you are not able to resolve and get in agreement with your spouse, it's time to seek help.

There is no shame in getting counsel. Getting counsel is simply allowing someone to look in on your situation and give you their input as to how they would handle it. In that process, many times new information and tools are acquired that you didn't have before. It doesn't make someone at fault, bad, or wrong. It's merely part of the process of growing and maturing.

Before we move on, let's deal with one more area: problems with the in-laws. Interestingly, this is where most of the attacks, accusations, and even enemies can come from. Obviously, there are a thousand scenarios that can be played out here. So, I'll just give some basic principles under which to operate.

1.) Each person leads in dealing with their own relatives.

Whoever has the relatives that are accusing or attacking should be the one to lead in dealing with them. From my experience, other approaches are not nearly as effective.

Guys, you lead in dealing with your family and relatives, and ladies, you lead in dealing with yours. Do not let them split or divide you so that you start publicly siding with the relatives against your spouse. That is not covenant.

2.) Families have pecking orders.

Someone is the big brother or sister, which in their mind puts them in charge somehow. Someone else is the victim or black sheep of the family, and they don't really have a say on things. Someone else may be the hero or the star of the family, and all attention revolves around them. Someone else is going to be the little brother or sister who doesn't really know much anyway.

Interestingly, these preconceived notions and expectations rarely seem to go away in a family structure, no matter how old the siblings are.

Here's my word of warning: if you ever hope to get resolution with in-laws and how they may view you, your spouse, or your marriage, you cannot allow yourself to fall back into the pecking order of the family and approach it from that mindset. It will not work. You need to accept each other as co-equal adults and discuss issues from that perspective. It will work the best and produce the best results.

The more people in the family can be objective and deal with the issue from a professional, business-like posture, the greater the chances are there will be resolution.

Sad to say, the parents are often the loose cannons in the mix. What I mean by that is too often, they can "go off" in any direction and take anybody's side. Worse yet, they may have their favorites, and everyone knows whose side they are going to take. They should be the most mature, predictable and stable in the group, but the more dysfunctional the siblings are, chances are the parents are also dysfunctional. They raised the family to be what it is. They may be the parents, but that doesn't mean they're always right or mature.

   3.) Huge family meetings usually don't work. Don't try to resolve with everybody at the same time. Not only will your issue be on the table, but all the issues they have with each other in that particular area will also come into play.

Often, it's better to deal with the siblings or parents one at a time. More progress is made that way.

   4.) Everyone needs to understand that once you make covenant with your spouse, that relationship is not open for everyone else to run.

That family unit must function between the two people who chose to get married and God. It's not anybody else's business to tell them how they should run their life, marriage, and family.

This may seem a little harsh, but some siblings or parents are very brazen, and they won't back off. In their minds, they have it settled that they will direct your life and business whether you like it or not. Here is where the true understanding of covenant comes in. Once we've made a covenant with our spouse, there is no other earthly relationship that is more important, comes before, or takes precedence over that covenant. Covenant means you have chosen to invest your life into that person and be loyal to them *first*. Everyone and everything else comes lower in priority.

I've seen situations where the couple had to literally tell some or all of the in-laws to back off, or they were going to withdraw from the family. Until things could be resolved, they would stay away from the family.

Is that right? Shouldn't family always come first?

No. Not in covenant.

A blood covenant relationship trumps any other type of human relationship. And God expects us to handle it that way.

Speaking of enemies in the family, the last group I want to touch on is the children. Children can be a major enemy to a marriage, especially if they are not biological children of both partners.

> *In the mindset of covenant, the marriage partner is <u>always</u> placed as the first priority.*

Children know what buttons to push and how to play their cards in an effort to get what they want. To do so, they often pit one parent against another. Scripturally speaking, that puts them into enemy status with the marriage covenant. Why? The covenant takes precedence over *any other human relationship on earth*. That includes children. We're never to side with a child and form an attitude against our spouse. If the child is bringing something up that is accurate and needs dealing with between you and your spouse, do it privately. Then get back to the child on what *the two of you* have decided. Don't have it out in front of or with the child. Keep your covenant between the two of you.

Here is something that is also very misunderstood: from God's perspective, when you made covenant with your marriage partner, you agreed that your children would come second in priority to that marriage relationship. For children from a previous marriage to come before the spouse is to break the covenant by putting them first and the spouse second, third, fourth, etc. If you entered into a marriage covenant, the spouse is to be placed first above the wishes and desires of your children. Otherwise, you will have huge marriage problems, because that's not how covenant was designed to function. One of the spouses will feel betrayed for the sake of the child or children.

This brings up a few points: (1.) this is a crucially important reason to know the person with whom you are entering into covenant before you marry them. You need to know how this person will fit into the picture of you and your children. If they are not a good fit, don't marry them. It usually doesn't work when we marry and hope everything works out ok later. (2.) your children need to understand that the covenant with your spouse will come before them. I know that's big, but if we do it any other way, it likely won't work, because it's no longer abiding by the rules of covenant.

In the mindset of covenant, the marriage partner is always placed as the first priority.

Step #6: Then an animal was killed and split in half. The pieces were arranged so that the two people making covenant could walk around and between the pieces in a figure 8 fashion. This was called the "walk of death." It signified that *each person was dying to what they were: their desires, goals, ambitions, and anything else that would ever cause any type of conflict between them, or hinder them from walking in complete harmony and becoming one.* Then each one would point at the pieces and declare that is what God should do to them (as was done to the pieces) if they were to ever break the covenant.

This step most typically shows up in the vows. Most vows will declare the person's love, desires, personal investment, and commitment level to the other person. The vows should also declare the person's dedication and commitment to the fulfillment of the other person. If the vow is scriptural, it will include some type of reference to being a lifelong commitment -- *till death do us part.*

With the vow comes the realization that this is a very serious thing, and it can carry some very serious repercussions if it is broken.

Once we have entered into a marriage covenant, we are no longer the same person. Both individuals will have to lose anything in their life, thinking, or attitudes that causes conflict between the covenant partners. This process is aptly referred to as "dying" to ourselves. Try not to misunderstand me here; we don't lose ourselves as a person. If we liked cars before we were married, chances are good we'll still like them after the marriage. If one enjoyed cooking or playing an instrument before we were married, that is still a part of the make-up of the person, and chances are high that they'll still enjoy it after they are married. The point I'm trying to make is that how I live, what I do, and the things I enjoy now have to include another person, and my life will need to be managed in such a way that it does not cause conflict in our marriage.

> *It is about two people coming together to blend their identities and strengths into a new union that produces individuals that are even stronger than they would be had they remained single.*

For example: if you like cars and have been accustomed to buying whatever car or truck you want -- adding whatever accessories you like, driving whenever and wherever you feel like it -- I can almost guarantee that some of that behavior will need to change or it will cause conflict. If you pull up with a different car or truck you bought without ever talking to your spouse about it, there will probably be trouble.

Remember: in covenant our focus comes off of ourselves, and it goes onto the other person. What can I do to meet their needs, fulfill them, and make their life the best it can be? In covenant, that comes before our personal comfort and desires. So, if you like vehicles, you would be wise to marry someone who likes vehicles too. It will make the marriage go much more smoothly, because you'll have interests that are in common. That person will be much more likely to support you in your vehicle desires and dreams. If you marry someone who can't stand the amount of money you spend on vehicles and is just waiting for the opportunity to wean you from that, guess what? Until they grasp the concept of investing their life into you and supporting your desires and dreams, your marriage is going to be a powder keg of trouble.

That was probably more of a guy example; here's a ladies' example. If you enjoyed certain hobbies, or spending certain days with friends or at a women's group, and you continue on after the marriage without taking him into consideration, the chances of trouble developing are very high. Your life is no longer your own to do with as you please. There is another person involved. Your identity is not the same as it was before the marriage. Without repeating the points I made in the previous paragraph, let me just say that all the things about your focus coming off yourself and now investing your life into your spouse is true for you too.

Again, it all goes back to Step #1 -- we would do well to know the other person very well and know what we're getting into so we can count the cost before we make this covenant. In some cases, the cost is too high, and the marriage should not take place.

There are aspects of how my wife and I live that I don't think either one of us would have if we were single (which I believe is true for every married couple on earth). But since we are in covenant, our first focus is not what we want as individuals; it's what is best for the other person. That's all part of making a covenant. It is no longer all about who you are and your identity. It is about two people coming together to blend their identities and strengths into a new union that produces individuals that are even stronger than they would be had they remained single.

The last thing I want to stress under this step is that anytime we demand that the other spouse submit to us or demand they do something our way, <u>we are not acting in agreement with covenant.</u> This is a companionship, not a father to child relationship. It's not our position to be bossing the other person around and demanding what they need to do for us. Too often I see men or women demanding, manipulating, controlling, or deceiving so they can get their way. That is not of God, nor is it how a covenant is lived out. It's a sign of the marriage being out of balance and needing some serious attention and maturing. Chances are very good that one spouse is the victim and the other is the abuser in the relationship. Neither one is of God. Remember: the foundational focus of covenant is "us serving them", not "them serving us".

Step #7: Then, while standing between the pieces, each person would cut their wrist or hand, and these would be joined in a symbol of mingling the blood with each other. This was the heart of establishing or cutting a blood covenant and it *symbolized becoming one.*

The symbolization of becoming one is found many times in a marriage ceremony. The addition of blood into the equation is what makes it a blood covenant. It is pictured during the public portion of the ceremony by taking the Lord's Supper (Communion). In the Western culture, the main aspect of becoming one where blood is a key ingredient takes place privately, even though, technically, it is still part of the marriage ceremony. It is the sexual joining aspect of the ceremony. As the couple engages in intercourse, the female's hymen is broken, and as a result of becoming one with the physical bodies, blood is discharged.

In ancient cultures, this was not always a private event, since the "token of blood" was about the only way of determining whether a woman was still a virgin or not. In many cases, there would be representatives from the family appointed to be witnesses of the consummation of the marriage. And in certain royalty situations, where the offspring needed to be of royal blood, the consummation was often a public event with many representatives of both sides of the families present. If the token of blood was found after intercourse, all was well. She had been a virgin, and the coming child would definitely be of royal blood. If the hymen had been broken, that was evidence that she was not a virgin and the entire wedding could be declared null and void. So, the blood of the woman at the consummation of the marriage was extremely important.

But hers is not the only blood that enters the equation. Hematospermia -- which is the presence of blood in the semen -- is actually a fairly common condition that has nothing to do with any health problems in the man. From the man's perspective, it is possible that he also contributes a small amount of blood at the time of intercourse.

Either way, this is considered the blood aspect of a marriage covenant. This is what makes it considered a blood covenant.

I would like to briefly address the issue of a woman's hymen. The reason we need to do that is for any women who did not have the usual discharge of blood at their first intercourse that indicates she was a virgin, and also for the women who actually were not virgins on their wedding night.

The medical community has proven that women can be born without a hymen, or it can also be broken from a hard fall or an accident. Even if a woman is a virgin at her marriage, it is possible that she may not have an intact hymen at the consummation of her marriage. There is also the possibility that she is not a virgin on her wedding night. Does that mean these women can no longer enter into a covenant with their husband? Let's look at this equally. What if the husband is not a virgin at the consummation of his marriage? Is he kept from establishing covenant with his wife?

The answer is to all of the questions is no. Even though this was a huge piece of the ancient wedding ceremony -- and it had to play out perfectly for the covenant to be valid -- in the time of our covenant with God (the New Testament Era), the thing that purifies us, keeps us pure, and makes it possible to fulfill any of the qualifications of any blood covenant in a marriage is the blood of Jesus. He is the one who supremely gave His blood for everything that is of God in which man can be involved.

In marriage, the blood of the human being is a picture or representation of the more important blood that was shed by Jesus. From a New Testament perspective, by faith a couple can still be joined in covenant, whether either of them were virgins or not, or whether their physical blood entered the picture or not. Every good thing we receive from God comes by faith. If they will agree in faith to be joined in covenant, God will join them together. Scripture says that God is the one who does the joining anyway (Matthew 19:6). So, if your circumstances were less than perfect for your marriage, don't feel badly. Simply ask God to forgive anything you did that was not correct, and ask Him to view you and your marriage through the blood of Jesus. Everything will be fine. You'll be in blood covenant with your spouse.

The thing I want you to take note of is that the steps we take in creating a marriage are reflections of the steps that form a covenant. Marriage is designed to be a covenant. Not everything in this physical world goes perfectly and smoothly, and some people may not be able to fulfill every physical facet of making a blood covenant with their spouse. That's the wonderful part of Jesus and His sacrifice for us. Through Jesus, no matter what we may be lacking, through Him it is supplied, and we are made perfect, just as if nothing were ever lacking ("justified" is the scriptural term that describes this).

Step #8: Ground, mud or sometimes gunpowder would be placed into the cut. This would cause a very definite scar. This was *a lasting sign of the covenant and an outward evidence that the person with the scar was in covenant with someone else.*

The Western culture no longer cuts the hand or the wrist, and then smears it with mud or gunpowder. But we still do have a very recognizable evidence or token of the covenant that was just made. Typically speaking, in a marriage it is the exchange of rings.

The wedding ring is the publicly visible sign that a person is in a marriage covenant. Whether this portion of the wedding ceremony is elaborate or fairly simple, it still accomplishes the same purpose. The ring can be expensive, or it can be cheap, and it will still accomplish the same purpose. It is the lasting and outward evidence of the covenant.

The ring will accomplish the same purpose as the scar in the hand. When someone sees the ring, they know the person is not single but is in covenant with someone.

Now, I realize in America, especially among the women, what kind of wedding ring someone gets is a big thing. Most commonly it needs a diamond -- preferably a large diamond. The more expensive the ring is or appears to be, the more he must love her. I've watched ladies goo and gosh over fancy and expensive rings. Then when someone has a less expensive ring, they'll say something like, "That's nice," and quickly change the subject to something else. In reality, the emphasis that is being placed on the *token* of covenant is not the covenant aspect of love; it's the "how expensive is it'" aspect -- which may or may not be love.

Now that we know what the ring actually stands for, I think it's funny how sidetracked we've gotten from what the token of covenant is really all about. In covenant, the wedding ring really has nothing to do with how much value is being placed on the woman or how much he loves her. It is merely the outward sign that this woman is in a marriage covenant with someone -- nothing more and nothing less.

I've seen situations where the wife is wearing a multiple-carat diamond on her hand, and I wouldn't give ten cents for their marriage. It's a disaster. All the money that was spent on the ring evidently didn't transfer over into real life when it came to living out the covenant that ring stands for. I've also seen couples where the woman had nothing more than a simple wedding band, and their relationship was so solid and mature, it would be worth millions if converted into currency. You can have an expensive or modest ring and end up with an awesome marriage, or it can be a disaster. The cost of the ring has nothing to do with it. It's working at and building the covenant that the ring represents that makes all the difference in the world.

While we're on subject of the ring or the token of the covenant, let me make one more observation. By now you've seen that in covenant, the man and woman are supposed to be making an equal exchange, each person giving 100% of themselves to the other and investing their whole being into their partner. Right? So, answer this question: why is it that the woman is expected to get the most expensive ring (token of covenant) possible, and whatever the man gets is almost guaranteed to be way, way less expensive? Why doesn't she invest into him what she expects him to invest into her? Right from the beginning we see the fact that the average American does not understand covenant. Why do I say that? Because they are breaking the rules of making a covenant right from the beginning. It's to be an equal exchange between the parties involved. Isn't it interesting how our traditions get in the way sometimes?

When it comes down to it, we may not fully understand it, but most of us do have an idea of what the ring represents. That's why if a spouse starts cheating on the other and goes looking to have an affair, they typically remove their ring while they are doing it. Why? They know that the ring means they are committed to another person. Just that knowledge in itself, if nurtured, would lead them into a fuller understanding of covenant.

> *The wedding ring is the publicly visible sign that a person is in a marriage covenant.*

Step #9: At this point, b*lessings would be spoken* as a result of fulfilling the covenant. *Curses were also spoken* which would take affect if the covenant was ever broken.

This is one area where I think Western culture is actually more in line with the New Testament in how a marriage ceremony is handled. The reason I say that is because in Galatians 3:13-14, it says that in Christ the curse has been removed. As believers, we should no longer be living under any curses. If you pay attention, during a typical wedding you will find either a prayer of blessing or a pronouncement of blessings. This can take place during the ceremony or at the reception. Usually we don't hear curses being openly spoken for breaking the marriage vows during a wedding ceremony. That's in line with the New Testament and the change that came because of Jesus becoming the curse for us. God doesn't want that marriage to be cursed. He's done everything He can so it will be blessed.

However, I will say this: whether curses are openly spoken or not, everyone knows that when marriage vows are broken, some very negative consequences follow. I have yet to see a situation where being put away and being legally divorced is a blessing to anyone's life. There are always some very negative, ugly consequences that follow a broken marriage.

From God's heart, speaking blessings is the only thing He wants to happen in a covenant. We know that because He specifically worked at removing all curses from having an affect on us.

Once the covenant is made and we are happily on our way in our marriage, it would do us well to remember that God wants it a blessed, not cursed, marriage. Typically, on the wedding day, it's all happiness, well wishes, and blessings between the couple. It's after they've been married and some of the challenges of life begin to show up that the curses begin to flow. We need to be very guarded in what we say to each other after we're married. Bless your partner to grow, mature, and prosper in every possible way. Say it with your mouth. It can only help them and you in the relationship. Cursing them will hurt them and you. Let me give you some examples:

I've heard people say things like,

> "Had I known this was what you were like, I wouldn't have married you," or "You are really messed up in that area. You have no idea what you're doing. How did I get into this mess?" Or I've even heard, "I wish I would have married (so and so), I wouldn't have all the trouble I have because of you."

Then I've seen it move into things being said such as,

> "You're an idiot."

I've heard spouses telling other people that their partner is a little off in the head, that they just don't get some things in life, or they'll list the other's weaknesses in front of a group of people.

I had one man introduce his wife to me by saying,

> "I'd like you to meet my wife (_____). She doesn't look like much, but I love her anyway."

I'll never forget one incident where a group of us were standing around and talking. One guy's wife brought up the fact that he's not very mechanical and a very poor handyman. She went on to list all the things in the house that were broken that he refused to take care of. I think she was trying to spur him on to action (in a negative way), but I could tell by the look on his face, it wasn't going to produce anything good.

Besides the look of embarrassment, he had the look that said,

"And now I'm going to do even less for you."

Guess what? Their marriage ended in divorce a few years later. Her cursing him didn't fix anything, but in reality helped break it further.

Telling your spouse they are stupid, worthless, a waste of time and energy, ugly, or fat will not improve anything in the marriage. It will always make it worse.

All of these type of things become curses to them. It begins forming their thinking and life in a negative manner.

Then there are the couples that go all out and literally curse each other. They say they wish something bad would happen to their spouse, maybe it would teach them a lesson. Or they'll say that some day _____ will happen (and they'll say something that is absolutely horrible -- something that if they said that when they were dating, the other person would have run from the relationship). They'll cuss each other out and be very demeaning, belittling, and devaluing.

Again a story comes to mind. My wife and I were at a conference, and in the middle of the night we woke up to screaming and a woman banging on the door of the room next to ours. She was cussing him out, screaming, telling him what a (<u>blank-blank</u>) loser he was, and he better (<u>blank-blank</u>) open the door. He refused to open the door, and she went on and on and on cussing and cursing him. It was at least 1/2 an hour. Finally he must have thought the police or someone was going to be called because of her ranting and raving, so he opened the door.

Then, we could hear them going after each other in the room -- just a little more quietly. I'd be surprised if they are still married. The things she said to him would be hard to get over. And of course, locking her out of the room wasn't the best idea either.

Why would partners do that to each other?

It's simple: they are in con- tract thinking. They expect- ed the marriage to go a cer- tain way, the partner to be a certain kind of person, or that they'd get something different out of the marriage than they are getting. It's contract thinking. They got into marriage expecting it would be a certain way.

> *All of these type of things become curses to them. It begins forming their thinking and life in a negative manner.*

Now it's not that way, and they are angry and feel ripped off. They are disappointed, angry, embarrassed, and frustrated, among a handful of other negative emotions. Out of their negative emotions and perspec- tives, they are lashing out at the other person. They're not saying and doing things for the betterment of the other, but saying and doing things that will tear them down or make them look bad.

That's cursing your partner.

It won't produce any good. It won't make their or your life any better. In fact, I guarantee it will make it worse in the long run. The sooner we can deal with the pool of negative that is going on inside of us -- and get back to handling the marriage like a covenant -- the more quickly that marriage will turn around.

Curses won't produce good; they only destroy. Blessing the other person is the only thing that will improve the situation. Find something good to say to them. The more we deal with our own negativity, the more positive we'll see. We married them for their strengths. Do we remember what they are? They're still there; we just can't see them very well, because we've become so focused on their weaknesses. If we re-adjust what we're concentrating on, we'll begin to see life and our partner from a whole different perspective.

Step #10: The two people involved in making the covenant would exchange names. This again signified *the exchange of identities and becoming one.*

Again, this is something that is very common in our culture. Someone either adds a name to their own, or there is a name change as the result of a marriage. Most commonly it is the surname (typically the last name) that is affected. In America, usually the woman takes the man's last name. However in true covenant, that is not correct. Since covenant is an equal exchange, true covenant has both partners exchanging their names in some fashion. Whether it's taking on each other's last names, or mixing and combining the names to make a new name, neither partner is to be left with their original name.

It again is showing the former person no longer exists. Even their name has changed. It shows that two people have taken on a new identity and changed their names as proof of it.

Step #11: A covenant meal was eaten. This signified that each person was *taking the other into their very being or life and becoming one.*

This step sometimes appears in the ceremony where the couple will serve Communion or The Lord's Supper to each other. It can also happen at the reception, which actually is still part of the wedding ceremony. From my understanding, it is the reception where this is to be fully seen. In covenant, once the ceremony was complete, the two people making covenant would celebrate by having a meal with the people who were there as witnesses. It was this meal that they would feed each other.

The closest tradition we have that resembles this is the wedding cake. Both partners give or feed each other a piece of the cake. Have you ever wondered where that tradition comes from? It represents covenant. It's part of the covenant meal. Although, in many cases, it is turned into a joke to see how much cake can be smeared on the other person's face, it actually is still a very serious portion of making the covenant. I would presume in those situations the realization of it still being a part of the wedding ceremony and creating a covenant is not understood. That's why it has turned into a joke.

If we were to try to replicate the original traditions of making a covenant, when it's time for the reception meal, the bride and groom would literally feed each other the entire meal. Again, it's representing our intentions and efforts to give our life to them so completely that even the things we need to sustain life (like food), we are giving to them. At the same time, the partner is receiving, or taking what is being offered as deeply into their life as possible. This makes the other person as much a part of us as possible through the giving (feeding) and receiving (eating) of the covenant meal.

Step #12: From that point on they were known as *friends*. That term signified that a blood covenant relationship had been formed.

Hopefully, they are also friends as we understand it in the Western culture. However, the true application of the term "friends" as it pertains to covenant no longer exists in our culture. We have substituted it with a different term: "married". Either way, it means the same thing: the terms speak of the people involved in a blood covenant.

As you can see, the picture of covenant is found all the way through our marriage ceremonies. Yet sadly, most of us who live in the Western culture don't understand what a covenant is. I would guess that the average married person would not be able to explain or describe what the term "covenant" means, much less how they created one when they were married.

Nevertheless, whether we realize it or not, two married individuals are in covenant with each other. There are specific responsibilities that accompany that covenant, the greatest being that the person with whom you are in covenant is considered and taken into account FIRST in all areas of your life. That's why there is such an emphasis on becoming one. The two people are to live and be as one unit on this earth, being in complete harmony and unity.

That's why so many marriages end in tragedy. Most couples don't realize they are in a covenant, nor do they have a clue how to make it work. It would be like taking a small child, putting them in a car and asking them to drive it. First off, they really don't have a clue what a car is or how it works. So when they try to drive it, we all know what's going to happen. This is an accident waiting to happen. We just don't know how bad the accident will be. The same thing happens in marriages every day. We don't know what we're in, much less how to make it work.

Now, here is an aspect of this marriage covenant that most people are not aware: _whenever that oneness and putting the other person first in every aspect of life is jeopardized, the covenant is also in jeopardy._

Covenants are broken when someone or something else takes the position of being FIRST in one of the partners' lives. Once something else is intentionally placed before the needs and desires of the covenant partner, the covenant is in danger of being broken.

From God's perspective, a marriage covenant is one of the most powerful unions that can be made. Why? Because two are becoming one. The goal is complete harmony, unity, and agreement. The resulting power in that is mind-blowing. Look at what Jesus said:

Matthew 18:19-20 (NIV - underline added)
[19] "Again, I tell you that if two of you on earth agree about anything you ask for, it will be done for you by my Father in heaven. [20] For where two or three come together in my name, there am I with them."

Spiritually, a husband and wife should be praying the most powerful prayers. They already live in covenant agreement and unity, right? As they go to God in agreement, anything they ask for will be done for them. And as they remain in agreement in the name of Jesus, He is always with them. Wow! Just understanding and living in that one aspect of covenant will change a lot of lives and marriages. That's why the kingdom of darkness fights marriages with such fervor. The biggest threat to the Devil is two people coming together in agreement. Covenant. Anything is possible for them. I doubt there is anything that scares him more than true agreement in a marriage.

It's that lack of understanding and failure to realize what we actually have been given in covenant that causes a lot of the problems in our marriages. Westerners tend to think more in "contract" terms. We know what a contract is, and as a result, we think a marriage is a contract and should be viewed through contract mentality. This causes us to totally miss the spiritual power and authority that is being offered to every married couple, if they would only get into covenant unity.

Since thinking in contracts is such a big issue for us in the Western world, in the next chapter we'll compare "covenant mentality" with "contract mentality".

I would guess that the average married person would not be able to explain or describe what the term "covenant" means, much less how they created one when they were married.

That's why so many marriages end in tragedy. Most couples don't realize they are in a covenant, nor do they have a clue how to make it work.

Covenant or Contract

Chapter 4

What is the difference between a covenant and a contract?

Even though both are agreements, the underlying purpose and nature of each is quite different. In fact, they are almost diametrically opposed to each other.

The Western world is most familiar with contracts. We use them on a daily basis. We have contracts for buying real estate and vehicles, obtaining credit cards, making bank loans, using online services, making financial investments, securing employment, going to the hospital, renting a car or a motel room, and on the list can go. We are swimming in contracts. It's no wonder we think with a contract mentality.

What is the purpose of a contract? They are designed to protect all parties involved for whatever the contract is written. It gives the contract holders certain rights that are enforceable in a court of law. It sets the expectations that are to be met and also the consequences of not meeting those expectations. It actually comes from the perspective of, "I don't trust you to follow through on what you are saying and agreeing to, so I want to protect myself with something that is legally enforceable."

Contracts intentionally keep the parties involved as separate individuals with their own particular rights. I'm going to repeat that: *contracts intentionally keep everyone as a separate entity with their own personal rights*. It's all about remaining the individual I am and being able to enforce it. Contracts emphasize remaining an individual and working with the others from the baseline of the agreement. That's important to note, because it produces a mentality that is totally different than a covenant.

Contracts are all written to protect our "interests". Everyone in a contract wants their interests protected and guaranteed. Somehow, this contract will benefit me and my life. If that isn't happening in a certain participant's mind, they won't sign the contract. Rule of thumb: *this contract has to be good for me.*

Now don't get me wrong, contracts definitely have their place. This world would be in chaos without them. The problem is that by their very nature, contracts are designed to be self-serving. They are selfish by nature. We learn to view transactions, agreements, promises, goals, plans, and practically everything else in life from that selfish, self-serving perspective. Not only in a contract, but in all aspects of life we develop an attitude that says, *"If this isn't going to somehow be for my benefit and serve me, I don't want anything to do with it."*

That approach may work well for agreeing on a contract, but it doesn't work at all in a marriage. Marriage is not built on a contract. It is built on a covenant.

So let's briefly refresh our understanding of a covenant. A covenant is also an agreement, but it isn't focused on what's best for me; its focus is on what is best for the person with whom I am in covenant. It is not designed to establish, protect, and preserve my rights; it's designed to create an agreement where I give my rights away. In covenant, I am trying to bond with you and become "one" in everything we do, not stay separate from you. Covenant is not built around what I can demand of others. It is built around the premise that I am willing and agreeing to give everything I am to the other. Covenants are not about my interests, protecting my rights, and receiving what I "deserve" or what will benefit me the most. Rule of thumb: *covenants are motivated by what I can do for the other person in the covenant.*

> *Covenant is not built around what I can demand of others. It is built around the premise that I am willing and agreeing to give everything I am to the other.*

Covenants not only blur the lines of individual rights, but in most instances those lines are removed. A covenant relationship is one where, at the very least, I place my desires, preferences, goals, and rights second to those of the one with whom I am in covenant. Ideally, covenants intentionally erase individuality and strive to form the two (or many) into one, everyone having the same purpose, goals, and focus. It's all about becoming one. Covenants emphasize releasing our individuality and becoming one with the person with whom you are in covenant.

There are expectations in covenants, but they revolve around serving the other party -- not my rights and how the other person can serve me, as in a contract. Covenants are created for the benefit of the other person. That is the mentality. It has to be shared and acted upon *equally* by everyone in the covenant, or the relationship will be a disaster. To truly be in covenant with someone, you must make yourself vulnerable. Contracts, on the other hand, are designed to remove any vulnerability.

Marriages were designed to be a covenant.

Malachi 2:14 (NIV -- underline added)
...It is because the LORD is acting as the witness between you and the
wife of your youth,... <u>she is your partner, the wife of your marriage</u>
<u>*covenant.*</u>

Matthew 19:4-6 (NIV -- underline added)
Haven't you read," he replied, "that at the beginning the Creator
'made them male and female,' and said, 'For this reason a man will
leave his father and mother and <u>be united to his wife, and the two will</u>
<u>*become one flesh'? So they are no longer two, but one flesh.*</u> *Therefore*
what God has joined together, let no one separate.

Genesis 2:23-24 (NIV - underline added)
The man said, "This is now <u>bone of my bones and flesh of my flesh;</u> she
shall be called 'woman,' for she was taken out of man." That is why a
man leaves his father and mother and is <u>united to his wife, and they</u>
<u>*become one flesh.*</u>

From the beginning, marriage was designed to bring two individuals together and make them one. That's the reason that God called it a covenant in Malachi 2. That's why when we try to set it up like a contract, it will fail.

And to make things even worse, most of us in the Western world have no understanding of covenant. So, in an effort to help us understand the differences, I will add a number of comparisons to what I've already said above that will hopefully help differentiate between the two.

Contracts are often made for a limited period of time.
Covenants are made for the life of the individual and can even span
    generations.

96

Contracts are typically constructed with a series of, "If this happens, then that will be the result."
Covenants are not built on if/then. They are built on the, "I am in this 100% " principle.

Contracts are designed primarily for my benefit, and we view the relationship from that perspective.
Covenants are designed primarily for the benefit of the other person, and we view the relationship from that perspective.

Contract thinking is built upon "getting" or "receiving" something if certain conditions are met.
Covenant thinking is built upon "giving" and "investing" without conditions.

Contracts strengthen individual identity.
Covenants form a new identity from the two.

Contract thinking says I expect you to give yourself to me for my best.
Covenant thinking says I am giving myself to you for your best.

Contracts are self-serving.
Covenants are designed to serve the other.

Contract thinking tries to find what is best for me.
Covenant thinking looks at the relationship from what is best for the other person.

Contracts are built on what each party owes the other.
- What you owe me, and what I owe you.
- What are my rights, and what are your rights.
- What can I demand and/or consider a breach of contract.

Covenants are built on the gift basis.
> - Who I am, what I have, whatever I will be -- I give to you as a gift.
> - The attitude going in is, "I choose to invest myself into this person." It's not dependent on what I get in return. It's a gift of me.

In contracts, we expect the other person to keep their end of the bargain and make my life good.

In covenant, I am the one who takes on the purpose of fulfilling the other person, making their desires and dreams come true, doing what I can to help them have the best, most successful life possible.

Contract thinking revolves around what the other party can do to make me and my life better.

Covenant mentality focuses on what I can do to serve the other person and make their life better.

In contracts, we invest for ourselves.
In covenant, we invest ourselves into the other.

In contracts, we expect the other to hold up their end of the deal we made. They had better come through for me and do what we agreed.

In covenants, our focus is on holding up our end of the deal for them. How can I serve you?

Contracts are made upon very conditional promises.
Covenants are made upon unconditional promises.

Contracts look at what I can get.
Covenants look at what I can give.

Contract thinking looks for an agreement or compromise that will work out the best for what I want.

Covenant thinking looks for a way to serve, fulfill, meet the needs and interests of the other person, and help things work out the best for what they want.

Contracts are typically built on conditions of meeting halfway.

Covenants are built on giving 100% of myself to the other.

Contract thinking focuses on securing one's own rights and how those rights can be enforced.

Covenant thinking places its rights second to doing everything it can to fulfill the other.

True contracts have no need for and are normally void of any type of love.

True covenant is based on an agape love type of thinking.

Contract thinking wants all cost, expense, and sacrifice to be made by the other person.

Covenant thinking realizes there will be a personal cost, expense, and sacrifice for the betterment of the other person.

Contract thinking is about the other person investing the agreed upon criteria into me.

Covenant thinking is about me investing everything I have and ever will have or be into the other person.

Contracts are viewed as temporary.

Covenants are viewed as permanent.

Contracts are viewed as breakable -- I can get out of this if needed.

Covenants are to be viewed as unbreakable -- no way of escape is in our mind.

Contract thinking focuses on the agreed upon or legal obligations to the other person and their obligations to me.

Covenant thinking does not view anything as a legal obligation. Every thing given and received is a gift.

In contract mentality, we exchange our words and promises. We're committed as long as_____ (you fill in the blank).

In covenant mentality, we exchange who we are (we're 100% "in" no matter what).

Contracts are made to gain legally enforceable power and rights in a situation.

Covenants are made to be of service to the other person, hence the giving away of personal rights.

Contract thinking looks for self-fulfillment.

Covenant thinking looks how it can fulfill the other person.

Contract thinking causes us to look at the weaknesses of the other person and how they are failing us. It typically causes us to be dissatisfied with our partner.

Covenant thinking causes us to look at the strengths they are giving in support of us. It causes us to be thankful for the partner we have.

Contract thinking comes from the mentality of what I have to do.

Covenant thinking comes from the mentality of I want to do.

As you can see, we need to stretch ourselves to even get a grasp on what covenant thinks, acts, and looks like.

When the principles of covenant are fully engaged and played out equally between two individuals, married or not, they will produce the most fulfilling and lasting relationships possible to the human race. Our goal when we are married is to WORK at maturing in our covenant with our spouse so that the longer we are together, the further we move away from contract mentality in the relationship. The reason I say WORK is because having a good marriage takes WORK. It would seem that most everything in our culture and society stacks the deck against having a covenant type of marriage. Intentional effort will be required if we are going to establish that type of relationship with our spouse. That will take WORK.

Covenant mentality and thinking expresses the heart of God toward any relationship. The principles are rooted and grounded in love. Covenant is the basis on which the marriage relationship was to function. But as we all know, it hasn't worked out exactly as God wanted. As a result, people don't always treat each other as they should. Hurts come. Betrayals happen. Marriages end.

> *When the principles of covenant are fully engaged and played out equally between two individuals, they will produce the most fulfilling and lasting relationships possible to the human race.*

So what does God think of that? Does it matter to Him? If so, what is the rest of the world to feel about broken and ended relationships? What is God's perspective of how the rest of us should view these damaged relationships and people -- especially as Christians?

With the concept of covenant being so untaught in our culture, a false concept of what a marriage is supposed to be has been developed and used as a means to abuse and dominate couples to force them to stay together no matter how bad the marriage may be. Religion has probably done the best job of twisting and perverting what covenant is about. Religious dominance, abuse, control and manipulation is in my opinion the greatest enemy of a true and Godly covenant. The reason I say that is because religion can be so deceptive. It makes it look like we're doing the right thing, but in reality it's not God's way at all.

It's a paradox. How can something that God designed (covenant) be hampered the most by religion? Isn't religion what connects us with God? Well, it's supposed to. But too often, the religious establishment has become very corrupt in areas. Why? Because it's made up of people who are very self-serving and corrupt. So, from my perspective, religion is often the center of the bad teaching and abuse that people experience when divorce is even considered. Religion will make keeping the institution of marriage intact of more importance than ministering to and meeting the needs of the individuals. That is backwards. It's supposed to be more about the people than the institution. But like everything else where tradition and religion rules on this earth, it makes a nice-looking outward presentation, but the heart of the people involved can be really putrid (Mark 7:6-9; Matthew 23:25-28).

When we apply all this to contract vs. covenant mentality or thinking, we really need to make an effort to be led by God in establishing a Godly marriage. Religion may help if we abide by all the rules and keep it looking good on the outside; but if that stops, religious people will crucify us. This can cause a conflict in how the spouses approach their marriage issues. One (or both) may be afraid to make the decisions that are needed to do what is best for the other person and their marriage, because they know it will be unacceptable to the religious establishment. By establishment I mean the people -- aunts, uncles, brothers, sisters, parents, friends, pastors, etc. -- and all their beliefs, doctrines, and rules. We already know these people will pick their rules and beliefs over truly loving us or investing into our welfare (unless of course we do everything they say -- then they're all for us. If we don't, they have little use for us.).

As a result of not wanting to cause problems, upset the family or church, lose friends, be criticized or pushed out, the couple decides to take the hypocritical route. They haven't resolved much at home. They have basically put the other person out of their lives in every area they can, so they can do their own thing, their own way. But in front of the "religious bunch," they put on the face of "everything is good" and "we are happy." In truth, this marriage is a disaster, and they're not address-ing the core issues because they want to keep it hidden from on-look-ers. Either they'll live a fake marriage that looks good on the outside, but all kinds of evil is happening inside, or eventually it will end in di-vorce. I'll explain that process in the next chapters. It's called putting the partner away. God absolutely hates it.

The sad part is that the church and the religious bunch actually helped push them that direction by being so concerned about the outward im-age -- reputation, what people will think of them if they get divorced, and how to make rules to prevent that from happening -- that the people get lost in the mix. The church and religious bunch just wants them to conform, make the problems go away, and not embarrass us.

Let me restate something here that is very important. If two (or more) individuals are not 100% equally engaged in covenant type of thinking, someone is going to be taken advantage of and abused. That is a simple obvious fact. Covenant principles do not work unless everyone in-volved in that covenant are engaged equally and fully. Covenant was never meant to have a dominator and a servant, an abuser and a victim, a controller and a follower. Covenant is designed to function the best under the concept of equality and servanthood.

So I repeat this again: both individuals in the marriage must be 100% engaged with covenant principles for these principles to work correctly in a marriage. If that is not the case, someone will be taken advantage of, controlled, and abused.

What religion has done is say that as long as two people are living under the same roof, showing up at church together, and filing jointly on their tax return, they are still married. They're in covenant. That is not correct. They may be still married in the eyes of the state, but it's not the state that we are to be the most concerned about. Are they still married or in covenant in the eyes of God? This may surprise you, but *just because a couple meets the man-made criteria of what a marriage is to look like that does not mean they are still in covenant or married from God's perspective.* From a contract perspective, they may still look good. From a covenant perspective, they may not be married at all -- even though they still look like it from the outside.

Let me give you an example of this that I've had to deal with multiple times over the years. In fact, it has come up a few times while I have been writing this book. One of the two partners, either the man or the woman, gets into an affair with another person and commits adultery. I think it's obvious to most anyone that at that point, the best interests of the

> *What religion has done is say that as long as two people are living under the same roof, showing up at church together, and filing jointly on their tax return, they are still married.*

covenant partner are not being placed first. The violated partner discovers the affair and brings it out in the open between the two. Abuse begins toward the innocent person. They are accused, blamed, ridiculed, belittled, put down, sometimes the verbal and emotional abuse turns physical, etc. The person in the affair makes it clear and declares that the covenant partner is not "first" to them anymore, and they never will be. From here the situation can go a thousand directions, but let's concentrate on the common thread that seems to run through most of these types of situations. The "religious expectations" are now that the victim is supposed to hold the marriage together and do whatever they can to not get a divorce, because as long as they stay together, at least they're not divorced. It's presented like divorce is the worst sin that can be committed.

But here is God's perspective on this whole situation: He's not coming from the angle of trying to keep them from filing for a divorce. He's coming from the perspective of what is happening with the covenant they made. From His perspective, the marriage is already over; the covenant has already been broken. It doesn't matter if the legal paperwork of divorce has been filed or not. Why does He see it that way? Because one of the covenant partners is no longer putting the other *first* in this relationship. They have made a willful choice to put them away for a different person. That breaks all the basic tenants of their covenant. The covenant is broken. The sin will not be in going to the courthouse and getting a "bill of divorcement." The sin has already been committed. It happened when one of the covenant partners decided to break their covenant oath with the other partner and place them second to another person (The concepts of putting away and bill of divorcement will be discussed in the next chapter.).

From God's perspective, this is over. To force one of the spouses to stay in this abusive, violating, destructive relationship is of no value to God. The damage is already done. The relationship is already broken.

To force the person to be further broken as an individual is contrary to God's heart and love for wanting the best for that person. It's contrary to the principles of God. It's a fruitless endeavor, because the reason they were together in the first place was because of the marriage covenant. That has ended, and unless they want to re-establish that covenant, for what purpose are we trying to keep them together? If children are involved, they usually become the reason offered to that question. They need to stay together for the children. Really?

> *But here is God's perspective on this whole situation: He's not coming from the angle of trying to keep them from "filing for a divorce." He's coming from the perspective of what is happening with the covenant they made.*

I remember a situation in which I was involved and trying to help bring restoration. The couple had a fairly large family and a very prosperous business. She was a stay at home mom, the children were always clean, neat, and appeared very well-behaved. They were leaders and an active part of their local church. Everything looked good from the outside, except he was very dominating, controlling, and abusive. She also was a very strong-willed, independent woman. As you can guess, this clashed from time to time. He wanted to make her into something she was not created or gifted to be. As a result, abuse entered the picture in an effort to force what he considered the "perfect" family. It was not only emotional and verbal, but it turned physical. He would do things like drag her across the room by her hair because she wouldn't obey him. He raped her and defiled her with various forms of sex in which she didn't want to participate. Life went on, and the problems that needed to be taken care of were never addressed -- from my perspective the reason for not dealing with the core issues was probably because of pride. They presented as such a perfect, Godly family. Casually looking in from the outside, a person would have never guessed what was going on behind closed doors. Well, you probably guessed it. It was only a matter of time before the whole thing came crashing down and they were divorced. She couldn't go on enduring the abuse, and it crashed in on them.

However, in the church, if someone is in that position and puts a legal end to the already broken covenant, most of the time, the church freaks out. How can it be that they're getting a divorce? The church people act like the paperwork is the deciding factor as to whether they will be considered married or not. So we put pressure on them to stay in it. We often disregard the abuse, trauma, and suffering that is taking place. Why? So we can hold some kind of religious standard against divorce? That's a travesty.

The standard against which the church needs to be standing is the sin that destroyed the covenant in the first place. But too often, we'll look the other way when we see things that indicate a serious problem in the relationship. The thinking is, *hopefully it'll work itself out.* And if the church is set up like a "good ol' boys' club" and the pastor is part of that club, the victim doesn't have a chance of getting a fair shake if they bring it out into the open. The "good ol' boys" will paint them black in an effort to protect their buddy, and probably themselves; because if the truth were know, they don't treat their spouses very well either. The thinking becomes, *as longs as they don't get a divorce, everything is still good.* That is the furthest thing from the truth. The true intervention should be taking place when the problem is just beginning, not once it's headed for the courts. The church tends to focus on the wrong issue, and it's sad.

Religion has created a set of false criteria that determines whether a marriage is acceptable, and the criteria too often revolves around whether there is a legal divorce or not. That is not the criteria that God sets. His criteria have to do with whether or not the covenant has been breached. That's the thing on which the church should focus.

Both individuals in the marriage must be 100% engaged with covenant principles for these principles to work correctly in a marriage.

If that is not the case, someone will be taken advantage of, controlled, and abused.

The Misunderstanding

Chapter 5

Most people, including Christians, don't understand what the Bible really has to say about the marriage covenant. We think we know, but most have never seen the truth of what the Word really says. I personally think the reason for that is grounded either in religious abuse, fear, and control of what happens in churches, families, etc., or the pastors, ministers, and the Bible colleges who educate them don't have a clue about covenant themselves. Either way, as a result the people are ignorant to the truth.

The Old Testament and the New Testament are in agreement on what I am going to share with you. Jesus understood it very plainly. To truly understand God's perspective on divorce, we need to understand how He sees it -- not how we may have been taught the church sees it.

The misunderstanding comes from the fact that the Bible uses different terms to describe divorce than we do. There are two separate words in the Old Testament -- as well as in the New Testament -- that some translations of the Bible have lumped together in the single word of "divorce". We will begin by separating these two words, giving their definitions, and making scriptural applications so we can more clearly understand what God is saying about this subject. This will show how different versions translate the two words that describe the divorce process, and you'll see how those words can be translated correctly and incorrectly.

The first thing we need to understand is that there is a difference between "putting away" a spouse and "divorcing" a spouse. There are two predominate words used in both the Old and New Testaments that most translations have translated as "divorce". Each of these words means something different. Even though they are both part of the same process, they are not speaking of the same thing. There is a third Hebrew word that is used a few times in connection with "putting away" or "sending away" a spouse. It is "garash". It is used in the following verses, but I didn't find that it offered any substantial help in dealing with the divorce issue as it pertains to us today. Feel free to look up these scriptures and draw your own conclusions.

Genesis 21:10   Leviticus 21:7, 14; 22:13
Numbers 30:9   Ezekiel 44:22
Hosea 9:15

We will place most of our focus on the main two words that are used in the Old Testament, and the two words used in the New Testament in connection with putting away and divorce.

In the Old Testament, the Hebrew word used for divorce or divorcement is "kereethooth". It is typically defined as a cutting off the bond of marriage by giving a bill or written document of divorce. It is found in the following scriptures: Deuteronomy 24:1, 3; Isaiah 50:1; Jeremiah 3:8.

In the New Testament, the Greek word used for divorce or divorcement is "apostasion". It is defined as a written document or a written bill of divorce. It is found in the following scriptures: Matthew 5:31; 19:7; Mark 10:4.

Both in the Old and New Testaments, those Hebrew and Greek words are referring to the legal paperwork that takes place at the courthouse when a couple is divorced.

However, there is another word used to help describe the process we know as divorce. It is not talking about a written document that says a couple is divorced; it is talking about the process that took place before they got the divorce paperwork. This is called putting away. Again, it is a separate word in both the Old and New Testaments.

In the Old Testament, the Hebrew word used for putting away is the word "shalach". It means to send or push someone or something away; put away; forsake; leave; let go; push away; to get rid of. It is found in the following scriptures as it deals with one spouse putting away another spouse: Deuteronomy 22:19, 29; 2 Samuel 13:15-20; Isaiah 50:1; Jeremiah 3:1, 8; Malachi 2:16.

In the New Testament, the Greek counterpart generally used for putting away is "apoluo". Again it is typically defined, to dismiss, release, let die, let go, send away, to bid depart. It is found in the following scriptures regarding marriage relationships: Matthew 1:19; 5:31, 32; 19:3, 7-9; Mark 10:2, 4, 11-12; Luke 16:18.

If you look up the definitions of both words, they also include the word "divorce" as part of the process that surrounds putting or sending away. This is true, but "divorce" is not the definition of either word. When I refer to these two words, I will most often define them as "put or putting away", even though there are other meanings to the words. The only reason I'm doing this is for simplification.

Apoluo should always be translated as "put or sent away" (or one of the other meanings it carries) – not as "divorce". Kenneth S. Wuest translated it correctly in *The New Testament, an Expanded Translation* as "dismissed" or "put away," but never "divorced". The American Standard Version translates it as "put away" (also correct). And the King James Version got it right 10 out of 11 times in the New Testament. The one place it was translated incorrectly was in Matthew 5:32. It was incorrectly translated "divorced" and not "put or sent away" as it should have been. The Greek word there is not "apostasion". It is "apoluo" which has nothing to do with giving a written divorce. It always deals with the "putting away" aspect. Since the KJV has been a standard for so many years, that one translation mistake has led to a lot of confusion and misunderstanding on the subject. Here is a literal translation of those two verses and how they should read:

Mt 5:31-32 (KJV – underline and bracketed added)
[31] It hath been said, Whosoever shall <u>put away</u> his wife, let him give her a <u>writing of divorcement</u>:
[32] But I say unto you, That whosoever shall <u>put away</u> his wife, saving for the cause of fornication, causeth her to commit adultery: and whosoever shall marry her that is <u>divorced</u> [that is <u>incorrect</u>, it should be <u>put away</u>)] committeth adultery.

> **The first thing we need to understand is that there is a difference between "putting away" a spouse and "divorcing" a spouse.**

In America, these two Greek words are not differentiated, but used interchangeably as what we have come to call divorce. However, only one of the words refers to what we are likely thinking of when we say divorce. When the average American refers to divorce, they are typically talking about going to court and having a marriage legally dissolved. This involves splitting the property, etc. This is what the Bible refers to as a "writing, document, certificate, or bill of divorce."

This may be the shocking part: I will show you from scripture that *this is not the part that God hates, nor what makes Him angry.* So, what is it that God hates, or makes Him angry? *It's the putting away part of the process.*

Look at it this way: there is always a common reason why marriages end and one receives divorce papers from the other person or court. What is that reason? It's what happened before the divorce papers were officially filed. What happened? One of the two partners (or both) mentally, emotionally, and spiritually made the decision to *put the other away*, which ultimately ended in the *writing of divorce*. Some scriptures also refer to the divorced partner as being "sent away," which is the physical culmination of the putting away process. The thing that breaks the covenant or marriage actually begins long before the paperwork for divorce is ever filed.

The scripture also indicates that the putting or sending away can happen after the legal certificate of divorce is issued. In those verses, I presume it should be translated "send" or "sending away", because it's talking about the physical split that takes place after the final paperwork is complete. I point that out because some scriptures state it as the certificate of divorce had been given, and then the putting away or sending away took place. Others don't put it in that order. So, be patient and look at all the scriptural references so you can see the full picture of the process.

So, what is God's perspective concerning the different aspects of these two words?

It's the mental, emotional, and spiritual aspect of the putting away process that God loathes. Why? Because the putting away is what breaks the covenant between the two people. The physical papers are merely the result of one or both having been put away by the other. It's the broken covenant that God hates, not the filing of papers or what we typically consider a "divorce". A common sense approach to the subject will tell us that the putting away portion is the bigger issue. Think about it: filing paperwork in the court system is a fairly recent event. For thousands of years, that was not possible, and people were still being divorced even though there was no paperwork at the courthouse. If filing the paperwork was the big deal, then why did God say in His Word that he hated the separation of a marriage even back then when there was no legal paperwork with the county or state? As far as the history of humans on this earth goes, there have been far more times when there was no county or state in existence, compared to the amount of time we've had courthouses, counties, and states. According to the Bible, God was upset back then when there was no courthouse. Why? Because the paperwork is not the big issue to God. It's the breaking of the covenant by putting the other person away that is the big deal to God.

In our society, we seem to put more emphasis on the divorce papers than on the broken covenant. That's not scripturally correct. Do you realize, it is possible to remain legally married in the eyes of society, when in reality the covenant has been broken? In God's eyes, once the marriage covenant is broken, there is no longer a

> *What is it that God hates, or makes Him angry?*
>
> *It's the "putting away" part of the process.*

marriage. But in the legal system's perspective -- or the public's perspective -- the two people are still married. Why is that? We're emphasizing the wrong thing. We are placing more emphasis on the physical paperwork and going to court to get a legal divorce than we're placing on the breaking of the covenant or the "putting away" that caused us to go to court and do the paperwork.

As we develop on this, you'll understand why this is important.

Let's begin by looking at what the Old Testament has to say about it.

Old Testament Scriptures

Chapter 6

We're going to take a close look at a number of scriptures so we can see what they are saying. Let's begin with the two words in the Old Testament that explain this process.

The first group of verses on which we'll focus contain the Hebrew word "kereethooth". This is the word that deals with a person giving a written document of divorce.

The first verses we'll look at are in Deuteronomy 24. The regulations around these verses have to do with the Old Testament law, which do not apply to us in the New Testament. But giving a person a written statement or bill of divorce is spoken of here as well as in the New Testament. This scripture is important to look at, because Jesus dealt with it and it does apply to us today.

Deuteronomy 24:1-4 (KJV -- underline and bracketed words added)
When a man hath taken a wife, and married her, and it come to pass that she find no favour in his eyes, because he hath found some uncleanness in her: then let him write her a bill of divorcement ["Kereethooth"], and give it in her hand, and send her out ["Shalach"] of his house. And when she is departed out of his house, she may go and be another man's wife. And if the latter husband hate

her, and write her a bill of divorcement, ["Kereethooth"] and giveth it in her hand, and sendeth her out ["Shalach"] of his house; or if the latter husband die, which took her to be his wife; Her former husband, which sent her away, may not take her again to be his wife, after that she is defiled; for that is abomination before the Lord: and thou shalt not cause the land to sin, which the Lord thy God giveth thee for an inheritance.

Deuteronomy 24:1-4 (NIV - underline and bracketed words added)
If a man marries a woman who becomes displeasing to him because he finds something indecent about her, and he writes her a certificate of divorce ["Kereethooth"], gives it to her and sends her from ["Shalach"] his house, and if after she leaves his house she becomes the wife of another man, and her second husband dislikes her and writes her a certificate of divorce, ["Kereethooth"], gives it to her and sends her from ["Shalach"] his house, or if he dies, then her first husband, who divorced her, is not allowed to marry her again after she has been defiled. That would be detestable in the eyes of the Lord. Do not bring sin upon the land the Lord your God is giving you as an inheritance.

Deuteronomy 24:1-3 (AMP - underline and bracketed words added)
[1] WHEN A man takes a wife and marries her, if then she finds no favor in his eyes because he has found some indecency in her, and he writes her a bill of divorce ["Kereethooth"], puts it in her hand, and sends her out ["Shalach"] of his house, [2] And when she departs out of his house she goes and marries another man, [3] And if the latter husband dislikes her and writes her a bill of divorce ["Kereethooth"] and puts it in her hand and sends her out ["Shalach"] of his house, or if the latter husband dies, who took her as his wife, ...

120

Let me immediately state that the law concerning remarrying someone from whom you have been divorced no longer applies to us in the New Testament. It was part of the Old Testament Law. But the part of giving a certificate of divorce to someone when they are sent away does apply, because it agrees with New Testament teaching.

I'd like it understood that there is a lot of history and cultural traditions woven into all the scriptures that deal with putting away and divorce. I am going to be explaining a lot of them in the next few pages. Then, as we look at other scriptures which either talk about them or refer to them, you'll already have the understanding of what is being said and why. Bear with me as I give the background information. It applies to these verses, but it also applies to the verses that follow.

In this section of scripture, even though our focus is on the bill of divorce, we have both Hebrew words in use referring to the divorce process. You find "kereethooth," which deals with the bill of divorce, and we also have "shalach," which is the word that shows the putting or sending away part of the process.

The putting away and divorce all hinges on her not finding favor with the husband, or some "uncleanness" that is found in her (KJV). It says that if after a couple is married, she "displeases" him (NIV) or he finds something "indecent" about her (NIV), he may give her a bill of divorce and put her away.

When we look at the word "uncleanness" or "indecent" in the Hebrew, we find these words are talking about figurative or literal nudity. There are two very different explanations.

One explanation has to do with a purely physical thing. Some feel it's referring to her having been sexually unfaithful to the husband and the discovery of the "indecency" of her not being a virgin. If she was not a virgin (according to the token of virginity or blood that had been collected at the time of their first intercourse), he would automatically have the right to put her away and divorce her. Others feel it's saying that if something about the woman when she is physically nude was displeasing to the husband, he could divorce her. Some take it even further by saying it refers to the mishandling of the bodily discharge during the monthly menstrual cycle, which may be displeasing or indecent to him. The bottom line was that something was wrong with her physically that the man didn't like.

The second explanation says that the nudity aspect does not apply to only the physical, but also to the spiritual covering of the husband. After considering the culture of the time, some researchers believe this is dealing with a woman who uncovered herself from the headship of her husband, therefore leaving her spiritually uncovered or nude. Therefore the nude aspect has to do with spiritual choices the woman made. It is feasible that this may be part of the big picture of what is being said here.

> *They began to be very lenient in their interpretations, and putting away and divorce were condoned for basically any reason.*

If she removed herself from his covering, in essence she was spiritually naked. How could a woman do that? By doing something that showed she was not being submissive to her husband, following him, or being respectful to him. Seemingly, this could play out in two ways: she could *actually* have done that; or, from the *husband's perspective*, she had done that.

The reason I'm pointing both of these out is because the original words used don't tell us exactly which theory is correct, so we are left to guess. The same thing happened with the Jewish teachers who read these verses. They didn't know exactly what God was saying. As a result, they began to be very lenient in their interpretations, and putting away and divorce were condoned for basically any reason.

Something to take note of here is that the scripture actually doesn't say anything about her virginity being an issue in this verse. That's important, because whether virginity was included or not, it wasn't specifically stated. My research says that because that scripture was vague and did not specifically state what the actual reasons for divorce were, the men of that time simply included whatever definition of uncleanness or indecency they desired. That substantially opened the door to being able to get rid of a wife for basically any reason they wanted to. Their application of the passage was that if a man was displeased with his wife sexually or in any other way, he could put her away and divorce her. The result: there were many reasons for *putting away* a wife and giving her a *bill of divorcement*. There is no definitive answer. However, the argument that says they made it much larger than simply a virgin issue is substantiated in Matthew 19:3 where the Pharisees asked Jesus the question, "Is it lawful for a man to divorce his wife for <u>any and every reason</u>?" In their minds, they had expanded getting a divorce to include basically any and every reason.

I'm going to touch this point again because of its importance. What happened that caused this passage to be used for so much harm? The problem was that the original Hebrew words were too vague. They didn't specifically say what the real problem was and why the husband could give her a divorce and send her away. This seems to be one of the main verses that Jewish men used when they were referring to divorcing their wives for "any and every cause" (Matthew 19:3). They said it that way because of the vagueness of this verse in detailing the reasons for putting away and divorce really had to be. They simply took the liberty of saying: it sounds like I can divorce her for any and every reason I'd like.

Either way, the husband had a very easy way out of the marriage. If he wanted her out -- no matter what she did -- he could simply say she was displeasing to him. The result: she'd be put away and divorced. Wow! Talk about a wife living in uncertainty concerning her future. She never knew whether she would be married and have a place to live or not. It all was determined simply by the whim of the man.

That's what the men were doing. They were putting away and divorcing for any and every reason. All the man needed was to find (the KJV says) "no favour" or "uncleanness" or something he "hates" in her. The NIV translates it as she "becomes displeasing" or he "finds something indecent" or "dislikes" something about her. The AMP says she "finds no favor" or he finds "some indecency" or something he "dislikes" in her. That is truly divorcing a wife for *any reason*. Just about anything could be classified as one of those things. Women were in a very bad situation in that time.

Obviously, the true victim here was the woman. She had no recourse in the situation whatsoever. In that culture, women had no legal rights. She was considered collateral or physical property of either her father or her husband. Women were literally bought and sold like cattle. She was truly at the mercy of anything her husband decided.

As parents watched this happen over and over to the daughters of their family, some of them wanted to find a way to stop it. Legally they had no recourse either. So, the parents of the bride began making marriage contracts ("ketubbah" -- discussed below) in an effort to stop it. However, because of the weakness of the laws -- as well as the disadvantageous standing a woman had in society in that time -- women continued to be abused, taken advantage of, and discarded by their husbands. (We'll discuss the "ketubbah" in more depth a bit later.)

This treatment of women got the attention of God. That's why He also stepped in and gave a law that protected the woman. God said, if you are going to put her away, then give her a divorce.

Deuteronomy 24:1-4 (KJV - underline and bracketed words added)
When a man hath taken a wife, and married her, and it come to pass that she find no favour in his eyes, because he hath found some un-cleanness in her: then let him write her a <u>*bill of divorcement*</u> *["Kereethooth"], and give it in her hand, and send her out ["Shalach"] of his house. And when she is departed out of his house, she may go and be another man's wife*

I'd like you to notice two things here: (1.) a written divorce paper was given, and (2.) the woman was sent away. This was the scenario and regulations on how this situation had to be handled from God's per-spective. It was put into the Old Testament Law. This is the way it was to be done. Why would God do that? Why would he make a law that said, if you are going to put her away, you must give her a written bill of divorce? Isn't God siding with the men here and giving them a way out?

I don't think so, and here's why I say that: there are times that what is happening on this sin-filled earth is horrible. Because of the need to let everything play out, God is not able to step in and change the whole system (at this time -- there is a day coming when He will). He's given the authority to run the system over to man. There are times He has to work within the ungodly system under which man has chosen to live. The result is that He must choose between the lesser of two evils. He can't step in and change the system into what He really wants it to be, so He picks the aspect of the system that will be the least damaging, and He goes with it. Let me show you an example of this. The following verses come from a story where God is getting ready to take the Israelites into the Promised Land. Notice what He says to them about why He chose to do what He did.

Deuteronomy 9:4-6 (NIV)
[4] After the LORD your God has driven them out before you, <u>do not say to yourself, "The LORD has brought me here to take possession of this land because of my righteousness." No, it is on account of the wickedness of these nations that the LORD is going to drive them out before you.</u> [5] <u>It is not because of your righteousness or your integrity</u> that you are going in to take possession of their land; <u>but on account of the wickedness of these nations,</u> the LORD your God will drive them out before you, to accomplish what he swore to your fathers, to Abraham, Isaac and Jacob. [6] <u>Understand, then, that it is not because of your righteousness that the LORD your God is giving you this good land to possess, for you are a stiff-necked (hard and stubborn -- AMP) people.</u>

God was not deciding to do something on the basis of right versus wrong. He's deciding on the basis of two reasons: (1.) He promised Abraham, Isaac, and Jacob that He would do this, and (2.) these people were so wicked, they needed to go. One of His major considerations for doing what He did was a choice between what's already bad and what's worse. He picked the lesser of two evils. God had told Abraham, Isaac, and Jacob that He would bring the people back to this land. Then He said something three times in these three verses. If we were to paraphrase it, the verses would sound something like this:

> (v. 4) It's not because you're so right that I'm going to drive out these enemies. In reality it's because of the wicked-

ness of these nations that I'm going to drive them out.

> (v. 5) Let me say it again: it's not because you are so right and have so much integrity that I'm giving you their land; it's because they are so wicked, and because I told Abraham, Isaac, and Jacob that I would.

> (v. 6) So understand this: it's not because of how good or righteous you are that I'm giving you this land, because in reality you are a hard ("hearted" -- Hebrews 3-4), stubborn, and stiff-necked bunch of people.

> *God picked the lessor of two evils.*

God is saying, I'm going to give you the land because these nations are worse than you. They are so wicked, they shouldn't be allowed to live like this any longer. That's why I'll drive them out of the land and give it to you. It's not because you are so right; you're both wrong! I chose to give you the land because they are worse than you.

As you can see in just that one example, God will make choices between what is bad and what is worse, because He's working with a fallen system, and about the only righteous thing He can do is to pick the better of the two bad situations.

That is what He's doing in Deuteronomy 24 regarding the marriage problems that were happening. It really is a drastic measure for God to take. If God had His way, neither putting away nor divorce would happen (Matthew 19:4-6). But God saw that what He wanted to happen in society wasn't going to happen for a long time, so He chose to do something that was better than not doing anything at all. What was it? He decided that rather than forcing a woman to stay in a marriage that was not marriage at all, he would make a way for her to get out. Hence the law: guys, if you put her away, then you will also divorce her. Was it really to protect the woman? Yes. As we look deeper at the culture of that time, we'll see more details as to why God did that.

For example: this was a time when polygamy was an acceptable practice in that part of the world. It was normal for a man to have multiple wives. The problem was that he was not always pleased with the one he had married. Now, I realize that can sound very chauvinistic. What about the woman's thoughts, feelings, desires, and whether she likes her husband? Doesn't she matter in all of this? In those times the answer actually was, no. Her opinions or feelings didn't matter much. Women were considered to be property and were purchased (dowry) from the family for a son to marry. It was the man's (or the parents') desires and opinions that mattered the most. Women had very little to say in the whole matter. It must have been a very horrible time for most women to live and be in marriage relationships.

Because of these things happening to their daughters, history tells us that some of the parents began creating a form of a marriage contract ("ketubbah") to try and protect their daughters from this type of abuse. Let's talk about that "ketubbah." This contract varied widely according to the desires and agreements between the parents or those making the contract. However, there seemed to always be a few items that were in included in every contract: (1.) dowry price, (2.) promise of virginity on the bride's part, (3.) the agreement of dissolution should the bride be found to not be a virgin at consummation, and (4.) the "bride price" or how much it would cost the groom should he give her a certificate of divorce for any reason other than her lack of virginity.

This was a very terrifying process for the woman. She not only had to pass the "virgin test," but she had to be accepted by the family. This stipulation was often included in the contract ("ketubbah"). In Deuteronomy 24 verse 1, it says if she doesn't find favor with him or displeases him, or if he finds some uncleanness or something indecent with her, or if he hates her -- he can divorce her and put her away.

Culturally, finding favor or being pleasing to the husband typically included the family's approval of her. If the future mother-in-law didn't like her, she was no longer considered pleasing to him. This was considered a pretty big loophole that allowed the man to get out of the marriage.

Something we need to keep in mind is: in that culture, once the couple was betrothed or engaged, they were considered married. So even if the wedding hadn't yet taken place, a divorce was required to get out of the marriage (eg: Joseph and Mary -- Matthew 1:19). During that engagement time, if the family didn't like her, it was considered equal to the future husband not liking her. This was because the family had the right to look out for the welfare of their son -- the future husband. At anytime during the betrothal or engagement, she could be put away or divorced if the groom's family didn't like her. This may seem shocking to us, but in truth the same thing still happens today. There are many couples who don't get married because of the disapproval of parents. The only difference is that today, we don't need a divorce to break up an engagement.

This was a very terrifying process for the woman.

An added aspect of this picture in Deuteronomy 24 is the physical "nudity" interpretation of the verse. With that interpretation, it allowed the "being displeasing" loop-hole to take place even after they were officially married. It was on the wedding day that he saw her "nude," so this was interpreted as saying even after the marriage -- whether immediately on the wedding night, or years down the road -- if any of the things above pertained to her, he could divorce her. Essentially, the man could put away the woman at any point in the marriage for basically any reason.

Let's go back to the culture of Deuteronomy 24. When a marriage ended in divorce, according to secular history, the groom and/or his family would often be required to pay the "bride price" for the marriage to be officially dissolved. It had been built into the marriage contract ("ketubbah"). Since in most cases this was pretty expensive, most husbands and families didn't want to have the financial hardship of divorcing the woman. Instead, they would stay legally married, and he would simply put her away. She was still legally married, so he didn't have to pay the bride price, but in the reality of what a marriage was intended to be -- she wasn't married. She had been put away or sent away from the position of being his wife. She was reduced to another random woman or housekeeper in the home. All the benefits of being in covenant with the husband were withheld. To make matters worse, he would often marry someone else, and the new woman would be the woman of the home. Wow! That's like rubbing salt in the wound.

In Matthew 19:7-8, Jesus gives us what He sees as the core of the problem with this picture. He pointed out that the whole thing was taking place because of the hardness of the man's heart. God's first intent was that no one would ever be put away in a marriage and it end in divorce. He wanted marriage to be for a lifetime. Yet after Adam and Eve sinned, that concept disintegrated pretty quickly. Even with sin imposing its will on mankind, God still didn't want a woman thrown out of the marriage -- especially for any and every reason (Mt. 19:3, 7). But men's hearts were hard, and too often it happened anyway.

I'm sure some of you are asking yourself: why would he marry some-one that he doesn't like or isn't pleasing to him? Again, look at the culture. Men married for multiple reasons: to make peace with enemies, as kinsman redeemer for a deceased brother or relative, for political advantage, to make covenant with a tribe or clan, etc. Not all marriages were even desired by the man or the woman. They were often viewed as marriages of necessity or profit. When the objective of the marriage was achieved, the woman was often put away, but not always divorced. The man would simply take other wives, and she would be ignored or treated as a slave in the household -- although still married.

Women were absolutely the target of abuse and were being taken advantage of, so in the regulations God lays out, He always requires a "writing of divorce" when someone was put away. In essence, God instituted divorce as a way out for the woman, because hard-hearted men are almost always abusive men. If the wife was no longer desired or wanted by him, she was in a living hell: rejected, despised, ridiculed, abused, set to the side, and simply put out of any interaction that would validate her as a married partner.

God saw that and was not happy about what was happening to the woman.

God saw that and was not happy about what was happening to the woman. In fact, this is the aspect of a marriage covenant breakdown that God hated -- when a woman was put away. This infuriated God.

God loved each and every woman who was being violated this way and determined that she was worth more than that. So He made a way of escape for her, rather than forcing her to stay in the abusive relationship (we'll show more scriptures on this later). He made a way out of that marriage for her. That way, she could at least go on with her life and start over.

There is a very important point we cannot miss, here. It is the fact that the husband was required to give her written paperwork stating that she was divorced (certificate of divorce). Why? According to this section of scripture (and others still to come), it was so she could remarry and not be in adultery. If he simply put her away, and she remarried, she would have been in adultery because she was still legally married. Until she was given a bill of divorce, she could not move on with her life and remarry. She was a prisoner, caught in a bad situation. God put this stipulation in the regulations regarding divorce as a protection for the woman. If she was caught in one of these unfortunate situations, she could get released from this marriage and move on with her life.

Please notice these two separate steps to the process. In our society, we would look at the whole thing as one step -- they got a divorce. God does not look at it that way. There are definitely two aspects to the process. Putting a woman away and giving her a certificate of divorce were two separate steps. In that culture, men were able to put their wives away, but they did not have to give them the certificate or paperwork of divorce. In other words, he could emotionally and physically put her away and treat her like they weren't married even though they remained legally married. He could marry other women or take on concubines and never legally divorce her with the correct paperwork. God didn't like it, so he made a law about it.

Remember, in the Old Testament era, polygamy was a common practice. Even many of those who we consider heroes or patriarchs had more than one wife -- men like Abraham, Jacob (Israel), David, and Solomon. The problem was that when a man would put away his wife for another, it would leave her trapped. She couldn't move on from that bad relationship. If she became involved with another man, she was in adultery, because legally she was still married. If she got re-married, she was in adultery because she was still legally married to the previous husband. She had no way out of the marriage. She was left with no recourse, no way of making the situation right. She was at the mercy of her husband. No matter what he decided, she had to go along with it. Women had no rights whatsoever unless something had been stipulated in the marriage agreement ("ketubbah"). She was reduced to property that he could do with as he pleased, no matter how it affected her. She was literally trapped and often reduced to nothing more than a slave in the relationship and the household, not only being treated that way by the husband, but also by the other wives he may take.

Josephus (a Jewish Historian) writes about it this way:

"He that desires to be divorced from his wife for any cause whatsoever (and many such causes happen among men) let him in writing give assurance that he will never use her as his wife any more; for by this means she may be at liberty to marry another husband, although before this bill of divorce be given, she is not to be permitted so to do." (The Life and Work of Flavius Josephus, Book IV, Ch. VIII, Sec. 23, line 154-155.)

It was God who stepped in and gave her some rights in a bad marriage situation. That point is really important because it's usually God who gets the blame for forcing a woman to stay in a bad situation no matter what. The term we hear is: "God hates divorce." Therefore they need to stay married no matter what's happening. It's not true. That's not God's character. He is the one who made a way of escape for the victim of a bad marriage. In the Old Testament, it was for the woman. In the New Testament, Jesus said it's for either of them (the man or the woman).

This concept and mistreatment of women is what infuriated God in the Old Testament and Jesus in the New Testament. Her value as an equal companion of the original creation was gone. This thing had degenerated into a philosophy where everything was about the man and his desires or choices. God was not happy with this, and His perspective was that if the man no longer wanted his wife, he needed to release her and allow her to move on with her life. But they weren't doing that. Why? Often, it involved financial reasons. It would cost him too much to legally divorce her (bride price). If the marriage was for political reasons -- or to make peace with a different tribe, clan, or nation -- it would be very detrimental to divorce her. It would have far reaching affects into the political and even international stage. So, the men would keep the marriage legally intact.

This degrading of women -- treating them like property to be used, discarded, or whatever -- infuriated Jesus. We'll see that in the next chapter. Even though the law of Deuteronomy 24:1-3 is a radical solution to irreconcilable marriage problems, it was valid then and is still valid today. When a divorce takes place, it severely damages the hope that the marriage can be saved, but it also puts an end to the abuse that is taking place in the relationship. It is a public statement that the marriage is over -- a very ugly ending to something that God had intended to be beautiful.

But remember: the true ugliness of the marriage ending didn't happen in the courthouse with the bill of divorce. It happened much earlier, behind closed doors and in the privacy of the marriage. Typically, the relationship had been falling apart and mishandled for a long time. The sin of the marriage dissolving actually happened when one of the partners was in the process of mentally, emotionally, and spiritually putting the other away (or both partners were putting each other away). The sin was not in the divorce papers. It was the putting away that broke the covenant, not the paperwork. That's why it's the putting away that God hates (Malachi 2:16).

If a marriage is going to be saved, the problem usually needs to be caught and helped in the putting away stage. Once it gets to the point where they are filing papers, the hurts, wounds, and pain are usually so deep that it's too late to do much. The trust has been so damaged, it would take a miracle to resolve. Don't get me wrong; resolution can happen. I'm just pointing out that the part of the process that the church and Christians tend to get all upset about (filing papers) is actually the wrong part. We're too late. We should have been involved and done something much sooner.

> *The mistreatment of women is what infuriated God in the Old Testament and Jesus in the New Testament.*
>
> *It was God who stepped in and gave her some rights in a bad marriage situation.*

Again I want to reinforce, the law of Deuteronomy 24:1-3 is actually an act of love and mercy on God's part. It releases people to move on in life and be free of the abuse they've been enduring. In comparison to simply being put away, the regulation (or command as it was stated in Matthew 19:7 and Mark 10:3) to give a written bill of divorce was God's declaration of the fact that women (or the victims) had value, too. They were worth saving from this horrible situation. Without that release from the relationship, they would continue on in the abuse (often followed by polygamy) and lack being valued as a spouse and partner.

As Jesus points out, it all stems back to one partner (or both) becoming hard-hearted (Matthew 19:8).

The situation of being put away but not divorced was a horrible situation in which to be trapped. It literally destroyed the future of the woman.

Let's look at another scripture.

Deuteronomy 22:13-29 (NIV - underline and bracketed Hebrew words added)
[13] If a man takes a wife and, after lying with her, dislikes her [14] and slanders her and gives her a bad name, saying, "I married this woman, but when I approached her, I did not find proof of her virginity," [15] then the girl's father and mother shall bring proof that she was a virgin to the town elders at the gate. [16] The girl's father will say to the elders, "I gave my daughter in marriage to this man, but he dislikes her. [17] Now he has slandered her and said, 'I did not find your daughter to be a virgin.' But here is the proof of my daughter's virginity." Then her parents shall display the cloth before the elders of the town, [18] and the elders shall take the man and punish him. [19] They shall fine him a hundred shekels of silver and give them to the girl's father, because this man has given an Israelite virgin a bad name. She shall continue to be his wife; he must not divorce ["Shalach," "put away"] her as long as he lives. [20] If, however, the charge is true and no proof of the girl's virginity can be found, [21] she shall be brought to the door of her father's house and there the men of her town shall stone her to death. She has done a disgraceful thing in Israel by being promiscuous while still in her father's house. You must purge the evil from among you. [22] If a man is found sleeping with another man's wife, both the man who slept with her and the woman must die. You must purge the evil from Israel. [23] If a man happens to meet in a

town a virgin pledged to be married and he sleeps with her, [24] you shall take both of them to the gate of that town and stone them to death —the girl because she was in a town and did not scream for help, and the man because he violated another man's wife. You must purge the evil from among you. [25] But if out in the country a man happens to meet a girl pledged to be married and rapes her, only the man who has done this shall die. [26] Do nothing to the girl; she has committed no sin deserving death. This case is like that of someone who attacks and murders his neighbor, [27] for the man found the girl out in the country, and though the betrothed girl screamed, there was no one to rescue her. [28] If a man happens to meet a virgin who is not pledged to be married and rapes her and they are discovered, [29] he shall pay the girl's father fifty shekels of silver. He must marry the girl, for he has violated her. He can never divorce ["Shalach," "put away"] her as long as he lives.

There are a number of regulations of the Law that are covered in this section of scripture. I added those scriptures that talk about them because they are a part of the overall context at which we're looking. However, just keep in mind -- those regulations do not apply under the New Testament.

The passage above was taken from the NIV Translation. As you can see, it translated it incorrectly. Instead of saying "divorce," it should have been translated, "put away". As you can see below, the KJV got it right. The specific verses I want us to look at are as follows:

Deuteronomy 22:19, 29 (KJV - underline added)
[19]..... and she shall be his wife; he may not put her away all his days.

[29] .... and she shall be his wife; because he hath humbled her, he may not put her away all his days.

Here we see the concept of "putting away." This is the word "shalach". The concept of divorce as we know it is not used in this passage. It is talking purely about putting the spouse away without giving them a certificate of divorce.

So let me point this out: putting a person away doesn't always follow the certificate of divorce in scripture. The certificate is not mentioned here at all like it was in Deuteronomy 24. This re-affirms two things: (1.) They are two separate steps in the process of breaking a covenant, and (2.) the putting or sending away can happen before, or even without, the certificate of divorce. This scripture is showing it is possible to put someone away without giving them a writing of divorce. However, scripture does not show the opposite where someone is given the certificate or writing of divorce without the person having been put away. I just wanted to point that out for clarification.

As I read this passage in Deuteronomy 22, I'm so glad we don't live under all the rules and regulations they had in the Old Testament. A lot of people would be losing their lives. The one thing that hasn't changed from the Old Testament is the breaking of a marriage covenant. God still views it the same today as He did back then. We'll see that when we get to the New Testament.

Another example can be found in the story of Tamar and Amnon.

2 Samuel 13:1-20 (NIV - emphasis & bracketed Hebrew words added)
[1] In the course of time, Amnon son of David fell in love with Tamar, the beautiful sister of Absalom son of David. [2] Amnon became frustrated to the point of illness on account of his sister Tamar, for she was a virgin, and it seemed impossible for him to do anything to her. [3] Now Amnon had a friend named Jonadab son of Shimeah, David's brother. Jonadab was a very shrewd man. [4] He asked Amnon, "Why

do you, the king's son, look so haggard morning after morning? Won't you tell me?" Amnon said to him, "I'm in love with Tamar, my brother Absalom's sister." [5] "Go to bed and pretend to be ill," Jonadab said. "When your father comes to see you, say to him, 'I would like my sister Tamar to come and give me something to eat. Let her prepare the food in my sight so I may watch her and then eat it from her hand.'" [6] So Amnon lay down and pretended to be ill. When the king came to see him, Amnon said to him, "I would like my sister Tamar to come and make some special bread in my sight, so I may eat from her hand." [7] David sent word to Tamar at the palace: "Go to the house of your brother Amnon and prepare some food for him." [8] So Tamar went to the house of her brother Amnon, who was lying down. She took some dough, kneaded it, made the bread in his sight and baked it. [9] Then she took the pan and served him the bread, but he refused to eat. "Send everyone out of here," Amnon said. So everyone left him. [10] Then Amnon said to Tamar, "Bring the food here into my bedroom so I may eat from your hand." And Tamar took the bread she had prepared and brought it to her brother Amnon in his bedroom. [11] But when she took it to him to eat, he grabbed her and said, "Come to bed with me, my sister." [12] "Don't, my brother!" she said to him. "Don't force me. Such a thing should not be done in Israel! Don't do this wicked thing. [13] What about me? Where could I get rid of my disgrace? And what about you? You would be like one of the wicked fools in Israel. Please speak to the king; he will not keep me from being married to you." [14] But he refused to listen to her, and since he was stronger than she, he raped her. [15] Then Amnon hated her with intense hatred. In fact, he hated her more than he had loved her. Amnon said to her, "Get up and get out!" [16] "No!" she said to him. "Sending me away ["shalach"] would be a greater wrong than what you have already done to me." But he refused to listen to her. [17] He called his personal servant and said, "Get this woman out of here and bolt the door after her." [18] So his servant put her out and bolted the door after her. She was wearing a richly ornamented robe, for this was the kind of garment the virgin daughters of the king wore. [19] Tamar put ashes on her head and tore the ornamented robe she was wearing. She put her hand on her head and went away, weeping aloud as she went. [20] Her brother Absalom said to her, "Has that Amnon, your brother, been with you? Be quiet now, my sister; he is your brother. Don't take this thing to heart." And Tamar lived in her brother Absalom's house, a desolate woman.

For clarification purposes: Amnon, Absalom, and Tamar all had the same father -- King David.

Here's the outline of the story. Amnon was in love with his half-sister Tamar. He wanted to have sex with her, so he devised a plan to make that happen. The result: Amnon raped Tamar -- his half sister (v. 14). According to Leviticus 18:9, this was sin. However, according to the scriptural laws of marriage in the Old Testament -- in certain cases, having sex with another was the act of joining in marriage (Deuteronomy 22:28-29). You might be thinking - but the Law didn't allow them to be married, because they were close relatives. That's true, but let me point out that the Law also stated that David and Bathsheba should have been put to death because of what happened between them (2 Samuel 11:1-5) according to the scripture above (Deuteronomy 22:22). Did that happen? No. So not everything took place as the law commanded. The point on which to focus is that from Tamar's and Absalom's (her brother's) perspective, what happened was actually a joining in marriage. However, because Tamar and Amnon were half-brother and sister, it was a very difficult situation that could have resulted in their deaths (Leviticus 20:17).

The story says that after they had sex, Amnon "hated her" (v. 15) and decided to put her away. At this point, Tamar makes a very interesting statement: "No!" she said to him. "Sending me away (the Hebrew word for putting away, "Shalach," is used) would be a greater wrong than what you have already done to me." What had he done? He had al-

140

ready sinned against her in such a way that they both could die. But she felt his next decision was even worse. Why? She knew exactly what he was doing -- he was putting her away. How could sending her out be worse? I believe Tamar realized he was dooming her to being alone the rest of her life, because she had been put away (v. 16).

Amnon wouldn't listen to her, and he put Tamar out (v. 17 - KJV & AMP). Absalom (Tamar's brother) also realized what had just happened and that she could not be married to anyone else unless Amnon would divorce her. To reveal that they had sinned would endanger their lives, so to help resolve Tamar's dilemma, Absalom offered to let her live with him. So Tamar remained desolate in her brother Absalom's house (v. 20 - KJV). Why? I think it was because Tamar felt she could not re-

> *She knew exactly what he was doing --*
> *he was putting her away.*

marry. She had been defiled, and she possibly even thought that she was already married. That's why she made the statement that if Amnon sent her out and away from him, it would be worse than the rape that had just happened. Was Tamar confused? We don't know for sure. But it's plain that as a young girl, she had been informed about being put away, and according to her own words, she obviously felt she had just become a victim of it.

Interestingly, if you read the rest of the chapter, you find that Absalom kills Amnon. The scripture says he was very angry with and hated Amnon because he had disgraced Tamar (v. 21). However, there might also be another reason he killed Amnon. This solved Tamar's problem.

With Amnon dead, according to the law, Tamar could again get married.

Here's another scripture where the two words for "putting away" and "divorce" are used:

Jeremiah 3:6-14 (NIV - underline & bracketed Hebrew words added)
[6] During the reign of King Josiah, the LORD said to me, "Have you seen what faithless Israel has done? She has gone up on every high hill and under every spreading tree and has committed adultery there. [7] I thought that after she had done all this she would return to me but she did not, and her unfaithful sister Judah saw it. [8] I gave faithless Israel her certificate of divorce ["Kereethooth"] and sent her away ["Shalach,"] because of all her adulteries. Yet I saw that her unfaithful sister Judah had no fear; she also went out and committed adultery. [9] Because Israel's immorality mattered so little to her, she defiled the land and committed adultery with stone and wood. [10] In spite of all this, her unfaithful sister Judah did not return to me with all her heart, but only in pretense," declares the LORD. [11] The LORD said to me, "Faithless Israel is more righteous than unfaithful Judah. [12] Go, proclaim this message toward the north: "'Return, faithless Israel,' declares the LORD, 'I will frown on you no longer, for I am merciful,' declares the LORD, 'I will not be angry forever. [13] Only acknowledge your guilt— you have rebelled against the LORD your God, you have scattered your favors to foreign gods under every spreading tree, and have not obeyed me,'" declares the LORD. [14] "Return, faithless people," declares the LORD, "for I am your husband....

Here we have a section of scripture that describes the fact that God put away and divorced Israel, and it tells us why He did it. He did it because, by their choices and actions, the people of Israel had broken the covenant with God. He wasn't first in their lives anymore. They had put Him away by making Him second to other gods. They started serving other gods. God compares this to adultery. He had clearly told them in the 10 commandments that in their covenant with Him, they were not allowed to have or serve other gods.

Exodus 20:3-5 (AMP)
[3] You shall have no other gods before or besides Me.
[4] You shall not make yourself any graven image [to worship it] or any likeness of anything that is in the heavens above, or that is in the earth beneath, or that is in the water under the earth;
[5] You shall not bow down yourself to them or serve them…

Israel initiated breaking the covenant with God through their spiritual adultery. That's why God reciprocated with sending her away with a "certificate of divorce" (v. 8). Please notice something here: Israel committed the sin when they put God away for other gods (committed adultery). Then God reciprocated and gave them a certificate of divorce and sent them away. Once Israel broke the covenant, God's response in ending the marriage by sending them away with the certificate of divorce was not sin. So, if a person is the victim of having been put away by their spouse, and they divorce and send the other person out of their lives -- they have not sinned with either action.

The interesting thing about this passage is that in the entire Bible, only one divorce is recorded between named individuals. It's in this passage. It was God's divorce. I think God did that in His word to make a statement about all the controversy surrounding divorce. If people were named, someone could take issue with what happened and discredit the example. But since it is God who is named, it silences the critics who would want to discredit it.

This is absolutely huge for a few reasons. First of all, we have a clear picture of God's heart on certain aspects of the whole process we call divorce. Secondly, it cannot be a sin to get a divorce -- because God got a divorce. God is a divorcee, and He cannot sin. Thirdly, God verified the two-step process involved in getting divorced. Fourth, it tells us what God's reasoning was concerning the marital problems with Israel and why He felt He needed to get a divorce. Let's look at these one at a time.

The first point: we have a clear picture of God's heart on certain aspects of the divorce process. Please get a grasp on this next statement: God understands marriage as well as divorce, and He's not nearly as con-demnatory towards divorce as many Christians and churches are. He has gone through both of them. God's own divorce shows us that there are times when God *does* think getting a divorce is necessary.

Which brings us to the second point: putting away and divorce are not always sin in God's perspective. Too often, Christians treat others (es-pecially other Christians) out of very ungodly attitudes and actions, and they feel justified because these people have stooped so low as to get a divorce. I've seen believers shunned by other believers and churches because they're divorced. In reality, the self-righteous attitudes and ac-tions coming from those looking in are as bad as any divorce. In cases of divorce for righteous reasons, (like God's divorce) the person with the poor attitude is actually the only one who is wrong in the situation -- not the divorcee.

The third point: God verified the two-step process of how a covenant is broken (putting away and certificate of divorce) as being legitimate and correct. How did He do that? He followed the precedent and did both steps. What we call "getting divorced" today is actually a two-part process: (1.) the legal certificate of divorce part, which happens in court, and (2.) the breaking of the covenant part, which is done by one

144

or both partners putting away the other person. The second part has nothing to do with court. It happens mentally, emotionally, and spiritually before the couple goes to court and is what actually causes the legal divorce to take place. Sending or putting away can also refer to the physical separations that take place after the divorce becomes legal in the courts.

> *God understands marriage as well as divorce, and He's not near as condemnatory towards divorce as many Christians and churches are.*
>
> *He has gone through both of them.*
>
> *God's own divorce shows us that there are times when God does think getting a divorce is necessary.*

The fourth point: from God's perspective, when it comes to marital unfaithfulness, putting away and divorce are absolutely justified. God compares worshipping something other than him (specifically false gods and idols) to be spiritual adultery. It's like having sex with a different person or lover. This point really drives home the covenant concept.

Why would God view it that way? Because He had a covenant with Israel (and Judah). That meant that He was to be first in their lives. He was to be loved, cared about, served, considered, and remained faithful to as the primary object of affection above anyone and anything else. When Israel pursued other gods, she put God away for a different lover.

145

She broke covenant with Him. God did not initiate the actions or the putting away that ultimately brought about the divorce; Israel did. Once it had taken place, God initiated the process of giving her a certificate of divorce and sending her away. She was no longer first to Him. God initiated and followed through on the divorce proceedings.

I remember when I was growing up, divorce very seldom happened in my circle of acquaintances. When it did, it was very important that the righteous person not file for the divorce first. That would help substantiate their innocence. If they filed first, somehow that made them the sinner. According to this scripture, the person who files first has nothing to do with innocence or guilt. In this example, God filed first, and He was totally innocent.

In the following scripture, God addresses the same problem:

Isaiah 50:1 (KJV - underline added)
"Thus saith the Lord, Where is the <u>bill of your mother's divorcement</u>, whom I have <u>put away</u>? or which of my creditors is it to whom I have sold you? Behold, for your iniquities have ye sold yourselves, and for your transgressions is your mother <u>put away</u>."

Isaiah 50:1 (NIV - underline added)
"This is what the LORD says: "Where is your mother's <u>certificate of divorce</u> with which <u>I sent her away</u>? Or to which of my creditors did I sell you? Because of your sins you were sold; because of your transgressions your mother was <u>sent away</u>."

Please notice: God put the blame for the broken marriage squarely on Israel. It was her transgressions that broke the covenant and the outcome of that was that God divorced her. She was the one at fault, not Him.

Are you seeing that in scripture, there is a clear difference between *putting away* and a *bill or certificate of divorce?* There is something very important which we must not miss here. Before the paperwork for divorce ever gets filed, there has been a putting away. The first step is always that one partner has been put away.

Here's a brief review to make sure we see this.

In the example in Deuteronomy 24, the man did the putting away of the wife because something about her did not please him. *When he mentally, emotionally, and spiritually broke from her and decided to get rid of her because of something that displeased him, this is when the first "putting away" actually took place.* This broke the covenant. That resulted in the second step of the process -- an official divorce and him sending her away.

In Deuteronomy 22, because of how the man had taken advantage of the woman, he was forbidden from ever *putting her away.* It said nothing of a *certificate of divorce.* In both cases (v. 19 & 29), since the man had already violated and mistreated the woman, he was not allowed to further violate her by marrying her and then simply *putting her away.* It didn't say anything about *legally divorcing* her. It said he couldn't *put her away.* This is important because it shows not only the differentiation between the two, but also that it is possible to put someone away without a legal certificate of divorce.

In 2 Samuel 13 we have the story of Amnon and Tamar. Again, he disgraced her and caused her to live a life of desolation because he *put her or sent her away* when he should have married her according to the law. Before she was raped, she even brought up the point that if he asked the king to marry her, she was sure the king would grant permission (v. 13). She knew this sexual encounter while she was still a virgin meant that they had to get married according to the law (v. 13). He didn't care, so he violated her, and then put her out of his life -- which according to Tamar was worse than the rape (v. 15-16). As a result, she couldn't get remarried as long as Amnon was alive. She was officially married to him. She lived as a desolate woman (v. 20), at least until Absalom killed Amnon (2 Samuel 13:28-29). After that, we do not read anything else about Tamar in the Bible. We don't know if she remarried or not, but according to the law, after Amnon was dead, she could legally marry again.

In Jeremiah 3, Israel was the one who broke faith with God by committing adultery. In covenant terms, Israel broke covenant with God by offering herself to others. *In covenant, this was the first putting away.* Israel had put God away from being her first love by giving attention to and choosing others. God responded to that by following the correct two-step process, which resulted in the certificate of divorce and him sending her away. The same perspective is mentioned in Isaiah 50.

This is important, because it shows that the broken covenant is what makes God angry -- not the written certificate of divorce or filing of paperwork. The paperwork comes about because someone has been put away. When two people come together in marriage, God joins them in covenant. As long as that covenant is intact, there will never be a need for a bill of divorce. But if the covenant is broken and one partner puts the other away, then the next step of giving a certificate of divorce is what God expects to take place.

Now let's look at this in the book of Malachi.

Malachi 2:10-16 (NIV)
"[10] Have we not all one Father? Did not one God create us? Why do we profane the covenant of our fathers by breaking faith with one another?"

Malachi was telling the people that the covenant they had with God was in jeopardy because they were breaking faith ("dealing treacherously" -- KJV) with each other. Please notice this: it wasn't God to whom they were being unfaithful; it was each other, and that put their covenant relationship with God in a jeopardy.

[11] Judah has broken faith. A detestable thing has been committed in Israel and in Jerusalem: Judah has desecrated the sanctuary the LORD loves, by marrying the daughter of a foreign god. [12] As for the man who does this, whoever he may be, may the LORD cut him off from the tents of Jacob—even though he brings offerings to the LORD Almighty.

Here, Judah's unfaithfulness is at issue. How have the people of Judah been unfaithful to God? By marrying women who worship foreign gods. Because of these marriages, the men were in sin against God. Malachi told them that God was going to remove them from the covenant He had with them (He points out Jacob as one of the ancestors of the covenant they had with God.). The reason they were going to be removed was because God had forbidden them from taking wives from other nations who didn't believe in the one and only God (Exodus 34:15-16). So in essence, the men were *breaking covenant* with God and *putting Him away* from being first in their lives by way of their disobedience. The result of that would be the loss of covenant with God.

[13] Another thing you do: You flood the Lord's altar with tears. You

weep and wail because he no longer looks with favor on your offerings or accepts them with pleasure from your hands. [14] You ask, "Why?" It is because the Lord is the witness between you and the wife of your youth. You have been unfaithful to her, though she is your partner, the wife of your marriage covenant.

Malachi goes on to tell them that God no longer accepts all their crying and offerings as favorable. They wanted to know why. Malachi's next statement is absolutely huge. He says the reason this is happening is because God is witnessing a problem between the men and their wives. *The men have been unfaithful to their wives, even though they had been in covenant with these women.* Evidently they had been married for quite some time, because the women were called the "wife of your youth."

The obvious question here is: was this an example of polygamy? Here's why I say that: seemingly they had been married for a long time. That was the person they were putting away. Were they putting away the wives of their youth because they had more recently married a woman who served foreign gods? The scripture doesn't definitively say, but it very well could have been the situation. If so, it is another example of putting away the first wife -- without giving her a bill of divorce -- and then marrying a second wife -- the exact thing that was making God angry. Let's go on to look at what the verses are definitely saying.

What we see here is a perfect example of two people being married, but one has been *put away* by the unfaithfulness of their partner. They have not officially divorced. No *certificate of divorce* has been given. They're still married, but the husband has been unfaithful. In other words, she has been *put away* for a different lover. God takes this so seriously that He threatens to cut them off from the covenant He has with the entire nation (v. 12). Watch how God develops this in the next few verses:

"[15] Has not [the LORD] made them one? In flesh and spirit they are his. And why one? Because he was seeking godly offspring. So guard yourself in your spirit, and do not break faith with the wife of your youth."

When someone is in a marriage covenant with another person, there is a dual joining and making one: (1.) "flesh," and (2.) "spirit". Godly off-spring come from being joined in both ways. Joining or being made one in the flesh (sexual intercourse) makes offspring. It's the spirit of mankind that is able to produce something Godly. Both are necessary to produce Godly offspring.

Then God emphasizes something: guard the spirit aspect of joining and becoming one in covenant. Don't break covenant (faith) with your wife. God goes on to address what he sees is really happening here:

"[16] "I hate <u>divorce</u>," ["Shalach" – "put away"] *says the LORD God of Israel, "and I hate a man's covering himself with violence as well as with his garment," says the LORD Almighty. So guard yourself in your spirit, and do not break faith."*

> ***The Hebrew word used in v. 16 for divorce is "shalach." <u>It means putting away. It does not mean giving a written certificate of divorce.</u>***

God says He hates "divorce." I've heard that quoted many times in reference to a married couple going to court and getting a bill or certificate of divorce, which says they are legally divorced. However, this is another one of the times the NIV translation has mis-translated this word. In my research, it appeared to me that most translations made the same mistake. Out of the 45+ translations that I checked, here were the ten that translated it correctly: Young's Literal Translation, Orthodox Jewish Bible, Authorized King James Version, 1599 Geneva Bible, Douay-Rheims 1899 American Edition, Darby Translation, BRG Bible, American Standard Version (ASV), 21st Century King James Version, and the Jubilee Bible 2000. The rest were incorrect.

The Hebrew word used in v. 16 for "divorce" is "shalach". It means *putting away*. It does not mean giving *a written certificate of divorce*. The word for a written certificate of divorce is "kereethooth". That is not the word used here. The word here is "shalach". To translate it using the word "divorce" is incorrect and misleading, because most everyone thinks it's referring to the legal certificate of divorce that we get at the courthouse. It is not referring to that document. *It's referring to the attitude in the man that led to the filing of the legal document*, the attitude that results in *putting away* a covenant partner. It's that wrong attitude that causes the couple to get the certificate or bill of divorcement. The KJV has it right:

Malachi 2:16 (KJV - underline added)
"For the Lord, the God of Israel, saith that <u>he hateth putting away:</u> for one covereth violence with his garment, saith the Lord of hosts: therefore take heed to your spirit, that ye deal not treacherously."

God hates it when a man *puts away* his wife (or in the time in which we live, that can be reversed to where the woman puts the man away). When a spouse does that to the other partner, they are breaking covenant with them and they are violating them. Like it says in v. 16, this is done in the spirit part of the person, emphasizing the fact that this begins within the person (mentally, emotionally, and spiritually) before it ever plays out in the physical. We need to guard against anything coming into the relationship that will cause one partner to develop an attitude with the other partner that literally puts them away.

We will discuss this in more depth, but let me say right here what *putting away* is about at its core. *Putting away is when we make covenant with someone, we enter into an agreement with them that states they will have first place in our life above anyone and anything else.* (Our personal relationship with God is the only thing that is excluded.) *When one of them puts the other away, they have chosen to place someone or something else at a higher priority than their spouse. That's breaking covenant. That's what God hates.*

The physical paperwork of divorce is simply the after affect of one having put the other away. That is not what makes God angry. In fact, the opposite is true. If one partner has put the other away, God says that they should give a bill of divorcement so the victim is free from the perpetrator's violence against them. That way, they can go on with their life and not live in perpetual bondage to the violation of the covenant.

> *If one partner has put the other away, God says that they should give a bill of divorcement so the victim is free from the perpetrator's violence against them.*

In v. 16, God said He hates putting away, as well as He hates "a man's covering himself with violence as well as with his garment" (NIV). This is a word picture. God is describing His perspective on the putting away. God hates it when a man violates a woman. Putting her away is violating her. "Covering himself with violence" has a dual meaning: it's referring to the violence he is inflicting on the spouse (since they are one, God sees it as violating himself.), and it can also refer to the violence he brought into the marriage and how it covers everything in that marriage (including himself) like a garment. Either way, God is very angry about it.

God chose a Hebrew word here that means to have such a personal hate for something that it is considered a personal enemy. God uses one of His names to back up His claim and give insight into what He is saying. He uses the name, "The Lord of Hosts" (KJV) -- Jehovah-Tsaba (v. 16). It means the Covenant God (Jehovah) of war, service, and the appointed time; to be of service and literally go to war (Tsaba). God is angry enough when this happens to a partner in a marriage covenant that He, as the God of Covenant, is ready to go to war on behalf of the innocent party. They have been violated through the breaking of the marriage covenant, and God hates it when that happens. That's pretty intense.

It has nothing to do with the *certificate of divorce*, which is the legal court process that Christians overemphasize. It has to do with the attitudes and actions happening in the marriage before the legal proceedings ever take place.

The certificate of divorce is not mentioned in Malachi 2. Again, it shows us that God doesn't hate the physical paperwork or *certificate of divorce*. He hates the *putting away* aspect of divorce, and He makes it very plain in this scripture that it's the *putting away* of a spouse that breaks the covenant -- not the paperwork.

There is one more aspect of Malachi 2 that needs to be pointed out. It's the word "treacherously". It appears in both the KJV and the AMP.

Here is how the Amplified Translation reads:

Malachi 2:14-16 (AMP - underline added)
[14] Yet you ask, Why does He reject it? Because the Lord was witness
[to the covenant made at your marriage] between you and the wife of
your youth, against whom you have dealt <u>treacherously</u> and to whom
you were faithless. Yet she is your companion and the wife of your
covenant [made by your marriage vows]. [15] And did not God make
[you and your wife] one [flesh]? Did not One make you and preserve
your spirit alive? And why [did God make you two] one? Because He
sought a godly offspring [from your union]. Therefore take heed to
yourselves, and let no one deal <u>treacherously</u> and be faithless to the
wife of his youth. [16] For the Lord, the God of Israel, says: I hate di-
vorce and marital separation and him who covers his garment [his
wife] with violence. Therefore keep a watch upon your spirit [that it
may be controlled by My Spirit], that you deal not <u>treacherously</u> and
faithlessly [with your marriage mate].

We've already seen in this passage that God is angry with how the men
were treating their wives, but what does dealing "treacherously" mean?
It's another word that God uses to describe what He sees happening in
marriages that needs to stop. Men were dealing with their wives in
"treacherous" ways. What does that mean?

In the following explanations and applications I'm going to apply these
scriptures both ways -- men to women, and women to men. I know it
doesn't read that way in the verses, but the reason I'm going to do it is
because in the New Testament, both Jesus and Paul make it plain that it
can happen from a woman to a man also. It isn't limited like it was in
the Old Testament where it's just the man dealing treacherously with
the woman. I think this is important, because it makes a more direct
application to the culture in which we are living.

In the original Hebrew language, to do something treacherously means to do things faithlessly, deceitfully, covertly, under cover, to violently rob and steal, to plunder.

I don't think this needs a lot of explanation. Just apply the definition to marriages that are having trouble, and it is pretty easily seen. Covertly and under cover means there were things going on behind closed doors that were not being brought out into the open. It could be called a dual-faced marriage. What you see when they wear their public face is not what is really happening when they are in private.

A New Testament description could include the word *hypocritical.* To be a hypocrite means to wear a mask or play a role. An aspect of a treacherous marriage is that it is a hypocritical marriage. In public, he is wearing a mask and playing a role of what the marriage is like; but if we knew what was really going on, it wouldn't look like what he presents in public. There is a covert and under cover life that goes on behind closed doors.

God is angry enough when this happens to a partner in a marriage covenant that He, as the God of Covenant, is ready to go to war on behalf of the innocent party.

They have been violated through the breaking of the marriage covenant, and God hates it when that happens.

What does that covert life look like? According to the definition of "treacherously", it includes faithlessness and deceit.This man or woman is not being loyal or faithful toward their spouse. They're living a deceitful life with each other. That can mean basically anything. It could be stealing money from the account, not being loyal with the spouse and the family financially, and lying about it. It could be that one is into drugs, gambling, an affair or something that is jeopardizing the family. They're not looking out for their partner's best in what they are doing, and they're lying about the things that are happening. They are not telling each other the whole story. You make the applications. It can go a thousand different directions. We do know they're not being faithful to each other, and there is deception as to what is really going on.

The last definition of "treacherously" is: to violently rob and steal, or plunder. Again, there are many applications as to what robbing and stealing from a spouse actually is -- but no matter what it is, they are plundering each other, and they're doing it violently. There is violence in the home. It could be emotional violence that is being used to control each other and is stealing their happiness, joy, hope, and freedom. It could be verbal violence, where one (or both) is being berated. It might include cussing and cursing, belittling, devaluing, and tearing the other apart with a violent tongue-lashing. It could also be physical abuse, where one (or both) is being violent with the other physically. Whatever that violence looks like, we know this much for sure -- it is stealing and robbing from each other. One or both are being diminished as a person in this relationship; and God hates it.

Again I repeat, I intentionally applied this to how it works in our culture, and because of what Jesus and Paul said, the putting away of a spouse can happen man to woman or woman to man. The word "treacherously" gave us an enlarged understanding of putting away and how it can work. So, to correctly apply Malachi 2 to our time, it can't

157

be only applied from the perspective of a man dealing treacherously with, violating, and putting away a woman. It must also be applied with the realization that a woman can do this to a man also (or they may be doing it to each other).

In those situations -- where one spouse is Godly and trying to do what is right, and the other is the perpetrator -- the perpetrator had better be careful. God hates what is going on and that one of the partners is being treated this way. He is so intense in His statement of hating it, that in v. 16, He used His name Jehovah-Tsaba to back up his hate for the putting away, violence and treachery that is happening to one of the spouses. Do you realize what that means? He's using the name that describes Him as the God of War. In other words, if the perpetrator pushes this thing too far, God Himself will step in to defend the innocent. Believe me, that is not a position in which *anyone* wants to be. Once God begins fighting against us, life can be really difficult.

As we look at these scriptures, are you seeing that God is more about loving and taking care of the person than He is about defending or upholding the institution of marriage? People are eternal. Marriage is not. Which one do you think means more to God?

Some may be thinking, but we can't just throw marriage and two people being committed to each other for life out the window. We can't act like it has no worth or meaning whatsoever. I agree with you. It needs to be held in high honor and regard. However, as we're doing that, let's make sure our focus is not simply trying to preserve the "institution of marriage". What really matters are the people who are involved. Keep the part that has the highest value (the people) as the highest priority. Don't throw the person under the bus to preserve the institution and keep it looking good in society's eyes.

Malachi 2 has been one of the favorite scriptures that I hear Christians quote: "God hates divorce." And their application is, you'd better not get divorced -- no matter what. God hates it, and if He hates it when people get a divorce, what do you think He feels and thinks about the person getting the divorce? Divorce is sin. No one should ever get a divorce. (And on and on the speech or sermon would go.)

Have you seen what this passage is really saying?

THIS PASSAGE DOESN'T SAY ANYTHING THAT EVEN RE-SEMBLES WHAT I WAS TAUGHT IT SAID. IT'S NOT EVEN RE-MOTELY TOUCHING "DIVORCE" AS WE UNDERSTAND IT IN MOST CHURCHES. THIS PASSAGE IS AGAINST A WOMAN BE-ING TREATED & HANDLED TREACHEROUSLY, VIOLENTLY, AND BEING PUT AWAY.

MALACHI 2 WAS WRITTEN TO DEFEND WOMEN (or anyone who is being treated like this in a marriage). It's not a threat to make us afraid of ever getting a divorce. It's a statement by Jehovah-Tsaba Him-self that says:

Pay attention and make sure You're right in what you're doing with your wives (spouses) and how you're treating them, or you will find yourself dealing with and answering to me. Because I hate it when a woman (spouse) is dealt with treacherously, violently, and then put away.

That's what is really being said in Malachi 2:10-16.

I know it was more of a cultural set-up of that time that put women in the position of being the one who was violated, but there is a bigger picture here than that. Satan doesn't like anybody -- he is filled with hate toward everyone. But I personally believe he hates women more than he hates men. It was through the woman that his ultimate defeat

159

was delivered. God prophesied it to him in Genesis when He said,

Genesis 3:14-15 (NIV)
[14] So the LORD God said to the serpent, "Because you have done this... [15] ... I will put enmity between you and the woman, and between your offspring and hers; he will crush your head, and you will strike his heel."

Right there, God said it: the woman and the serpent (Satan) will be enemies, and her offspring would crush his head. That offspring was Jesus, and He did exactly that.

Even though our culture is different in the Western world today, the warning to not abuse and mistreat the woman still stands.

1 Peter 3:7 (NIV)
[7] Husbands, in the same way be considerate as you live with your wives, and treat them with respect as the weaker partner and as heirs with you of the gracious gift of life, so that nothing will hinder your prayers.

The woman is the more vulnerable one in the relationship. Husbands, realize that, and treat her accordingly. If you don't, just like in Malachi 2, you will find yourself dealing with God through hindered prayers and not inheriting the life that God has for you. God is still defending women, even in the New Testament.

Before we go to the New Testament scriptures, let's restate a few things.

In the Old Testament, "putting away » is the Hebrew word, "shalach".

It is found in the following scriptures:

a. In regard to one spouse toward another:
- Deuteronomy 22:19, 29; 24:1, 3, 4,
- II Samuel 13:15-20   - 1 Chronicles 8:8
- Isaiah 50:1   - Jeremiah 3:1, 8
- Malachi 2:16

b. In other applications:
- Genesis 3:22; 8:9; 19:10   - Exodus 4:4; 22:5, 8, 11
- Numbers 5:2-4   - Deuteronomy 25:11
- Judges 3:21; 5:26; 6:21   - I Kings 13:4
- I Samuel 14:27; 17:49;   - II Kings 6:7
- II Samuel 6:6; 15:5; 18:12; 22:17; 24:10
- I Chronicles 13:9-10   - Job 1:11-12; 2:5; 29:9
- Psalms 55:20; 125:3   - Song of Solomon 5:4
- Isaiah 58:9   - Ezekiel 8:3, 17
- Joel 3:13

In the Old Testament, "divorcement" in the Hebrew is, "kereethooth". It is found in the following scriptures:

- Deuteronomy 24:1, 3
- Isaiah 50:1
- Jeremiah 3:8

There is another word used to describe the *putting away* element of a marriage breakup. It is the Hebrew word "garash". It is used in a few of the places in scripture where a putting away, driving out, or sending away of a spouse has taken place. Here is the list of references where it is used in conjunction to a marriage being dissolved.

- Genesis 21:10   - Leviticus 21:7, 14; 22:13
- Numbers 30:9   - Ezekiel 44:22

The last word that is used to describe the same process is, "yatsa". In connection to marriage, it is found in the following verses:

- Ezra 10:3, 11, 19

Now let's look at this concept in the New Testament.

New Testament Scriptures

Chapter 7

In the New Testament, we also find two words that describe the same process as in the Old Testament. The concept carries through pretty much intact.

To *put someone away* is exactly what it sounds like. It can be explained as simply as,

The process of moving or forcing
something or someone away from you.

That can happen spiritually, emotionally, mentally, and/or physically. To *put away* in marriage is to put someone out of your life.

The Greek word for *putting away* is, "apoluo". It is defined as, sending someone away; to dismiss, release, or free someone; to let them go. When you take that concept and compare it to what a covenant marriage is suppose to be like, you see that the covenant is damaged at best and broken at its worst. The person is no longer placed in the position of being first. They have been removed from that position, and someone or something else has replaced them. They have been released, dismissed, or sent away from that covenant position.

This is the action that God hates. The marriage covenant partner should always be considered first before anything or anyone else (besides God). Their opinions, feelings, and desires, should carry the most importance of any and all input. When that changes and someone is put in the second, third, or even lower position in a relationship, the covenant begins to feel the stress of that; and if not corrected, God considers it a breach of covenant. The covenant is broken between the individuals involved.

That is the beginning of the breakdown of the marriage. If the attitude remains unchecked, the marriage will likely dissolve through getting a divorce in the legal court system. It wasn't the document of divorce that was the problem. It was the attitudes and actions that were carried out in the putting away process that caused the final outcome.

"Apoluo" - the New Testament Greek word for putting away -- is found in the following scriptures:

   a. In connection to divorce:
     - Matthew 1:19; 5:31, 32; 19:3, 7-9
     - Mark 10:2, 4, 11-12
     - Luke 16:18

   b. In other applications:
     - Matthew 14:15,22 (cf. Mark 6:36, 45; Luke 9:12); 15:23, 32, 39; 18:27 (cf. Luke 6:37); 27:15, 17, 21, 26.
     - Mark 8:3, 9; 15:6, 9, 11, 15.
     - Luke 2:29; 8:38; 13:12; 14:4; 22:68; 23:16-18, 20, 22, 25. (cf. John 18:39)
     - John 19:10, 12. (cf. Acts 3:13)
     - Acts 4:21, 23, 40; 13:3; 15:30, 33; 16:35; 17:9; 19:41; 23:22; 26:32; 28:25.
     - Hebrews 13:23

Now, let's look at the other Greek word that is used in connection with this process.

The other Greek word in the New Testament that is often translated "divorce" is, "apostasion". This is the word that refers to the legal document or certificate given when a couple is divorced.

Biblically speaking, to fully or properly divorce someone, the putting away portion needs to be followed by the legal portion. Giving the legal piece of paper verifies what has already taken place in the putting away process. It is the piece of paper that verifies the covenant is broken. In our culture, this would take place at the courthouse.

The Greek definition for "apostasion" can be summarized as writing or bill of divorce; the legal papers that declare the end of a marriage.

"Apostasion" -- the New Testament word for the legal process or the bill / papers of divorce -- is found in the following scriptures:

- Matthew 5:31; 19:7.
- Mark 10:4.

We're going to look at four sections of scripture where Jesus deals with the subject of putting away and divorce. You will notice that I will repeat some of the main points -- numerous times. The reason I'm doing that is because they are contrary to the church's tradition view-point, which means they are probably the opposite of what you've been taught to believe. If I say something just once, it may not really take hold inside of you; so I am purposely repeating myself at times.

Let's begin with Matthew 5.

Mt 5:31-32 (NIV - underline and bracketed Greek words added)

"It has been said, 'Anyone who <u>divorces</u> ["Apoluo" -- "put away"] his wife must give her a <u>certificate of divorce.</u>' ["Apostasion"] But I tell you that anyone who <u>divorces</u> ["Apoluo" -- "put away"] his wife, except for marital unfaithfulness, causes her to become an adulteress, and anyone who marries the <u>divorced</u> ["Apoluo" -- "put away"] woman commits adultery."

This passage of scripture appears in what we call the Sermon on the Mount. In it, Jesus touches many subjects, one of which is divorce and remarriage. The above passage was quoted from the NIV Translation, and as you can see, they incorrectly translated "apoluo." It does not mean "divorce". It means to "put away." The KJV does a better job on this verse.

Mt 5:31-32 (KJV - underline and bracketed Greek words added)
It hath been said, Whosoever shall <u>put away</u> his wife, let him give her a <u>writing of divorcement</u>: But I say unto you, That whosoever shall <u>put away</u> his wife, saving for the cause of fornication, causeth her to commit adultery: and whosoever shall marry her that is <u>divorced</u> ["Apoluo" -- "put away"] committeth adultery.

As you can see, the translators got it right the first two times, but the KJV also mis-translates "apoluo" at the end of verse 32. The word there should not be divorced; it should be the phrase put away. These errors in translation have caused the confusion among many believers. The result is that putting away and divorce have been seen as the same thing, and they are not.

As we go into these passages in the New Testament, let me note something to which you should pay attention: Jesus used a form of the word "apoluo" eleven times in these verses in the gospels. In every passage we study, Jesus was against "apoluo" (putting away), but not once did He indicate that giving a "apostasion" (certificate or writing of divorce) was wrong, which is almost the opposite of what Christians believe today.

As you can see in Matthew 5:31-32, Jesus is not against giving a writing of divorce. He is against putting someone away without giving the legal divorce document. In fact, He agrees with the Old Testament Law by adding explanation to it. Jesus couldn't have contradicted the law like some people have said; if He were contradicting it, He couldn't have fulfilled it. He would be saying the law was wrong. We know that didn't happen. So what is He saying? He's saying if someone is going to *put away* his wife, *let him* give her a writing of divorcement.

The words "let him" do not carry the same connotation as in our present use of those words. Our application would be, "it's ok," or "it's alright" if he gives the divorce. In the original language, it is saying that if he's going to put her away, he is to follow through and also give her a divorce. It's not a suggestion. It's the correct order of procedure that needs to be carried out once a woman is put away. That's why in the NIV and the AMP it is translated, whoever puts someone away "MUST" give her a certificate or writing of divorce (divorce papers; legal divorce). The reason the NIV and AMP agree on the word "must" is because of the forcefulness of the original Greek word being used. The word "let" gives the inference that they can but don't have to. The word "must" says it needs to be done. (Compare Matthew 19:7 and Mark 10:3-4 where they use the word "command.") By bringing up that scripture (Deut. 24:1), Jesus is agreeing with it. Then in verse 32, He gives further explanation.

Before we go to v. 32, let's remind ourselves of some things. There were many reasons in Jesus' time that women were put away but not divorced. They were still doing what we read about in the Old Testament. Depending upon what the original contract drawn up before the marriage stipulated, the financial costs to divorce someone could become very high, so in many cases, they didn't give a legal writing of divorce. Instead, they would put the woman away and simply not treat her as a companion in the relationship. In many cases, she was often ignored and even replaced by another wife. Since multiple wives, or polygamy, was still common in that cultural time, putting away one wife and adding another was not a social disgrace.

Just like we read about in the Old Testament, the wife who was put away found herself living in a relationship and a household where she wasn't wanted. Often she became no more than a slave to serve the household and family. Jesus absolutely did not condone this. This is the same thing that upset God in the Old Testament. From God's perspective, not only is the victim robbed of a fulfilling marriage, but they are also prohibited from establishing a different relationship, which could become a good marriage. In verse 31, Jesus said if you're going to put her away, give her a divorce. Why would He say that? We know one reason is because He's quoting Deuteronomy 24. He agrees with it which means Jesus also wants to see the woman be able to move on with her life and not have to live under the abuse and violation of a husband who doesn't want her.

If the husband doesn't give her a divorce, they are legally married. If she starts another marriage or sexual relationship with someone else, she and the person involved with her are in adultery. She's still married. She has been put away, but not legally divorced. This is what God was talking about in Malachi 2 as He states how He hates it when a man covers his wife with violence. From God's perspective, this is violating the woman.

Again, for clarification I need to point out that in their culture, it was not possible for a woman to initiate a divorce with her husband. Only he could do that. That's why it's almost always written as the man divorcing or putting away the wife.

In v. 32, Jesus goes on with the explanation to give them further understanding. Before we read the next verse, let me give you a heads up: Jesus is not limiting the right to put a partner away to their having been involved in fornication or sexual marital unfaithfulness, like it has been widely taught. He is actually saying something totally different. I know that is often the common understanding of this verse among believers, so pay attention to what it's really saying. It may surprise you. It's not saying that the ONLY REASON a divorce is Ok is if a partner is sexually unfaithful or commits adultery. I know, that's what many of us were taught -- but it's not saying that. I'll prove that to you once we've looked at the scripture.

> *Jesus is not limiting the right to put a partner away to their having been involved in fornication or sexual marital unfaithfulness, like it has been widely taught.*

So, what is Jesus saying? Well, what is the thought on which He's expanding? It's in v. 31 -- if you're going to put someone away, to do it the right way, you need to give a certificate of divorce. Then in v. 32 He explains why He said that. Let's look at it with the original words in place.

[31] 'It has been said, 'Anyone who <u>puts away</u> ["apoluo"] his wife must give her a <u>certificate of divorce</u>.' ["apostasion"] [32] But I tell you that anyone who <u>puts away</u> ["apoluo"] his wife, except for marital unfaithfulness, causes her to become an adulteress, and anyone who marries the <u>put away</u> ["apoluo"] woman commits adultery.'

Now please re-read the verses above. To understand this, you will need to have a clear separation in your mind between what has been traditionally considered divorce verses put away. In this verse, Jesus is focused on the putting away aspect of the process and how that relates to the divorce (paperwork) aspect. Why is He focused that way? Because He's teaching about marriage, and if it's going to be dissolved, there is a correct process for doing it. He's answering why and when a "writing of divorcement" (KJV) is needed. He's not contradicting the law (Deuteronomy 24); He's giving clarification to it.

In v. 31, He said,

Mt 5:31 (KJV - underline added)
It hath been said, Whosoever shall put away his wife, let him ("must" NIV & AMP) give her a writing of divorcement:

Here the verse says that anytime someone is put away, they should be legally divorced (given a writing of divorcement). Keep that in mind as we look at v. 32.

We need to look at v. 32 from two different aspects, because Jesus is explaining v. 31, and He also adds an exception to His explanation. He's making two different points. We'll look at the explanation first, and then we'll look at the exception He adds.

Here is the verse:

(underline and bracketed Greek words have been added)
[32] But I tell you that anyone who put away ["apoluo"] his wife, except for marital unfaithfulness, causes her to become an adulteress, and anyone who marries the put away ["apoluo"] woman commits adultery.

172

Since we're dealing with just the explanation first, I'm going to show you that verse with the exception removed. Then we'll add it back in later.

[32] But I tell you that anyone who puts away ["apoluo"] his wife... causes her to become an adulteress, and anyone who marries the put away ["apoluo"] woman commits adultery."

Jesus will make this more plain to see in Matthew 19, but when we remove the "exception", He's clearly talking about putting someone away and re-marriage *when* THERE HAD NOT BEEN ANY UNFAITH-FULNESS.

If a woman has only been put away from a marriage (but not divorced), and she gets remarried, both her and the new husband are in adultery. Why? She isn't legally divorced. She's still married to the first husband. That's why Jesus agrees with v. 31 where it says if you are going to put away a spouse, you must give them a writing of divorcement. If the legal paperwork aspect of the divorce doesn't happen, the husband who put her away is actually guilty of causing her to commit adultery with another man. Why? He refused to give her a legal divorce, so she's still married to him.

I know this may shock some believers because of what we've been taught about getting a divorce, but read those two verses for what they are really saying. *Jesus is not condemning someone who gets a divorce. He's saying if the marriage is going to fall apart anyway, make sure it's done the right way. If you don't, from God's perspective, you're actually causing the other person to sin by committing adultery should they remarry.* He is not saying that a legal divorce is wrong, nor is He saying remarriage is wrong. He's saying that if someone gets remarried without out a proper legal divorce, *that* is wrong and will cause them to sin.

This is why what Jesus said in v. 32 is huge in our culture and time:

Getting divorced and then remarrying does not make a person guilty of adultery in God's eyes. It never has. Even in the Old Testament, it didn't say that. The belief or doctrine that most churches have that says if you get divorced you have to stay single -- you can never remarry. because if you do, you'll be in adultery -- that belief or doctrine is wrong. That's not what Jesus was saying.

Again I repeat: Jesus was saying that if you are only put away but not divorced, and you remarry (or get into an affair), you and the person you marry are in adultery. If you get a legal divorce and then remarry, you are not in adultery because you're no longer married to the former spouse.

The points Jesus is making here -- WITHOUT THE EXCEPTION -- are repeated and very easy to see in Mark 10 and Luke 16. I will point it out when we get to those scriptures.

> *So this belief or doctrine that most churches have that says, if you get divorced you have to stay single. You can never remarry. Because if you do, you'll be in adultery. That belief or doctrine is wrong.*

You may do well to stop right here and go over this a few times so you can fully digest what Jesus just said. Let it really sink in.

Now let's go on to the exception that Jesus added in his explanation. Now He's going to talk about putting someone away _when there_ HAD BEEN unfaithfulness.

Interestingly, Jesus adds clarification to this by saying that _when there_ HAD BEEN unfaithfulness, the certificate or writing of divorce is not needed. So from God's perspective, there is one situation where the legal paperwork doesn't matter at all. It's when someone had been unfaithful.

Now I need to say something: we live under a government that requires court proceedings to get a divorce for any and every reason. Don't take Jesus' statement and apply it to our governmental laws. In America, if we don't go through the legal process of filing for divorce in the court system, you may be OK with God according to the exception in v. 32, but you will likely get in trouble with the government. So with that said, let's look at v. 32.

(Underline and bracketed original Greek words have been added - exception is also underlined)
[32] But I tell you that anyone who puts away ["apoluo"] his wife, except for marital unfaithfulness, causes her to become an adulteress, and anyone who marries the put away ["apoluo"] woman commits adultery."

"Marital unfaithfulness" is generally believed to refer to sexual unfaithfulness in the marriage. Now notice: Jesus is saying that a partner CAN "put away" the other spouse -- _without giving them a legal divorce_ -- if that spouse has been sexually unfaithful and it will not cause an adultery issue. Why did he say that? It is because of the marital unfaithfulness exception. Should that spouse -- who was sexually unfaithful, or had committed adultery -- go on and marry another person, the one who put them away will not be causing them to commit adultery. Why? Because the unfaithful spouse had already committed adultery by being unfaithful. The covenant was already broken. It was broken when the unfaithful spouse committed adultery. There was no concern about future adultery, because they had already committed it. In those situations, the person (in this scripture, the husband) who puts the other away is not guilty of any sin -- even when they ignore the legal paperwork (remember: this was permissible in their culture, not ours).

That was huge in their culture because it released the husband from paying the bride price or making any financial restitution to her family. Her act of being sexually unfaithful released the husband from any pre-arranged marriage agreements or contracts. He could simply put her away and not give the legal paperwork of divorce.

If we take a serious look at that, it makes sense. Jesus was clarifying the fact that it wasn't the husband who was unfaithful. Why should he be financially punished or punished in any other way for the wife's infidelity? He shouldn't. That's not being fair to him. So Jesus clarified that point.

So now let's look at the church's traditional interpretation of this verse and show why there is so much confusion and error concerning what Jesus really was saying.

Here is what I've come to understand is the church's traditional interpretation of v. 32:

> Divorce is wrong. If you divorce and get remarried, you will be in adultery. The only exception to that is if your partner has committed adultery and has been unfaithful. If that happened, you can get a divorce and remarry and it's Ok. You won't be in adultery in the second marriage. But if adultery hasn't happened, you can't get divorced and be right before God. You must stay in that marriage no matter what. Jesus said you can't get a divorce.

First of all, before I prove to you why that interpretation is wrong, let me point out the obvious thing in that traditional interpretation that is already wrong and will mess with everything else: it's the word divorce. The word "divorce" does not appear in v. 32. When believers or the church use it there, they are already in error. The word is "put away". By now you know the difference between the two. They are not interchangeable, nor do they mean the same thing. Verse 32 is not talking about getting a divorce; it's talking about one partner putting the other away and then remarrying. So already the traditional belief I listed above is in error. It's that traditional viewpoint which uses the word divorce that messes up the meaning of the entire verse.

But it goes deeper than that.

Secondly, There's no stipulation that Jesus laid out that says there's only one way you can get divorced and remarried: it's if there has been unfaithfulness. HE'S NOT TALKING ABOUT *"DIVORCE AND RE-MARRIAGE"*. HE'S TALKING ABOUT *"BEING PUT AWAY AND REMARRIAGE"*. It's not an exception that says there's only one way that God approves of divorce and remarriage. It's an exception that explains the one reason that God approved of someone getting remarried without a divorce. If there had been unfaithfulness, Jesus said it was Ok to put them away and not give them a written divorce. THAT'S HIS WHOLE POINT.

The church totally misunderstands this scripture, and the traditional interpretation is almost the exact opposite of what Jesus was saying. Jesus is not talking about forcing someone to stay in a marriage because they haven't met the qualifications to get a divorce. He's talking about how someone can get out of a marriage. There is a correct and incorrect way of doing it.

His thought is still on v. 31, which said that to do a marriage breakup correctly, it needed to be fair to all parties. When someone has been put away, they need to be given a written divorce. He's simply explaining it. His explanation adds an exception to that rule. The only exception that DID NOT require a written divorce to be given when a marriage broke up was when there had been unfaithfulness. Then, no written divorce was needed before a remarriage. That was the exception.

> *Jesus is not talking about forcing someone to stay in a marriage because they haven't met the qualifications to get a divorce. He's talking about how someone can get out of a marriage.*

Remember: the issue in that culture was not trying to find a way to keep the couple together. That was already happening, and as a result of it, the women were being abused. The problem in their culture was forcing the husband to give the wife a divorce. They were refusing to do it. So, Jesus isn't saying what our culture interprets this verse as: you must stay together EXCEPT for one thing -- if there has been unfaithfulness. He's saying the exact opposite. He's saying if someone is put away, get a divorce and move on in life. The only reason a divorce is not needed to move on in life and remarry is when one partner has been unfaithful. Then you don't need a certificate of divorce; just move on in life.

Again, I strongly restate: the ability to remarry without a legal divorce applied to their culture -- not ours. You will be breaking the law if you do it that way in our culture.

Hopefully you've seen what Jesus was really saying, but if not, I said

I'd prove to you why our traditional interpretation is wrong. So now I'll do that. It revolves around the belief that if we get a divorce and remarry, we are going to be living in adultery. I'll do it by giving a hypothetical example. Again, remember that Jesus wasn't talking about divorce in v. 32. We've added that concept. He was talking about putting away. That correct interpretation is KEY to my next example.

> *Remember: the issue in that culture was not trying to find a way to keep the couple together.*
>
> *The problem of their culture was forcing the husband to give the wife a divorce.*

Let's say I put away my wife for some reason (whatever reason -- it doesn't matter what the reason is. Just note that it WAS NOT because of unfaithfulness). I've put her away, and she is no longer first in my life. I don't consider her desires or opinions very much. I've decided to live my life the way I want to, and I don't care what she thinks. As a result, she may also have gotten frustrated and decided to live her life without me. We have separate friends, activities, interests, etc. About the only thing we do together is live under the same roof -- and maybe we don't even do that anymore. She lives someplace else. My point is: obviously this covenant is broken. I put her away first, and then she may or may not have reciprocated on it and put me away too. I just haven't followed the process through and gotten a divorce.

Here's the big question -- in that hypothetical example:

How did my putting her away cause her to commit adultery?

It's true: we are living separate lives, and I've put her away, but:

How did my putting her away cause her to commit adultery?

IT DIDN'T! In this example let's re-emphasize: the fact is that neither one of us has been with another man or woman. There hasn't been any sexual activity with anyone other than the person we're still married to -- each other. There hasn't been any adultery in the example. So I ask the question again:

How did my putting her away cause her to commit adultery?

Again I say: IT DIDN'T!

You might be thinking, why would I ask that question? Here's why: it has to do with the misconception of the church that says "divorce" and "putting away" are the same thing, so we interchange them. We use the word divorce in that verse -- which isn't correct. As a result we say that if a man divorces his wife, if she remarries he's caused her to commit adultery.

> *If Jesus would have used the word "divorce" in v. 32, that interpretation and belief would be correct.   But the word isn't "divorce" -- it's "put away".   That's what makes that belief incorrect.*

I know many couples where one or both have put the other away. They are still legally married. Neither one has become involved with another person. They live under the same roof, but live separate lives. Has the "putting away" caused one of them to be in adultery? No.

However, if they do what Jesus was saying they shouldn't do -- which is to just go and get remarried without the legal divorce -- THEN THAT PERSON IS IN ADULTERY. They're still legally married to the first spouse. The second marriage is simply an adulterous affair.

That's what the average Christian has been taught and believes. If we divorce someone, and there hasn't been unfaithfulness in the marriage, we are causing them to commit adultery, and anyone marrying them will be in adultery. THAT IS NOT WHAT JESUS SAID!

This explains why bad translations have really messed up and confused this subject. If we would have been taught what Jesus *actually said* about this verse, rather than something He *did not say*, divorce and re-marriage would be a very easily understood subject. Most ministers are still teaching these verses incorrectly, so the average person has a huge amount of bad teaching, which has produced numerous incorrect belief systems. It's no wonder the church is so messed up when it comes to this subject.

So, for sake of discussion, how could the adultery issue have gotten into the picture in the hypothetical example I just gave about my wife and I? Here's how: if I would have put away my wife -- BUT NOT DI-VORCED her -- and she remarried without getting the certificate of divorce, then adultery would have entered the picture.

Jesus said it in v. 32:

(Underline has been added)
[32] But I tell you that anyone who puts away his wife, except for marital unfaithfulness, <u>causes her to become an adulteress, and anyone who marries the put away woman commits adultery.</u>"

Adultery gets in the picture if we remarry without being legally divorced.

If we remarry WITHOUT THE CERTIFICATE OF DIVORCE, we're in adultery. However, there is no adultery if we have been legally divorced, because at that point we're no longer married to each other. Jesus is saying the same thing as Deuteronomy 24. The only difference is that He added an exception to protect the innocent party if there has been marital unfaithfulness or adultery while the two were still married.

The church's traditional interpretation actually has it backwards. JESUS IS NOT FORBIDDING DIVORCE EXCEPT FOR ONE REASON -- UNFAITHFULNESS. HE IS ACTUALLY SAYING THAT WHEN SOMEONE HAS BEEN PUT AWAY AND THE COVENANT HAS BEEN BROKEN, THERE NEEDS TO BE A DIVORCE! IF THERE ISN'T ONE, IT WILL CAUSE AN ADULTEROUS SITUATION.

This point is so big and contradictory to what has traditionally been taught by the church in America, I think we need to review what we just learned from Matthew 5:31-32.

The first point Jesus was making is that IF THE WOMAN WAS NOT UNFAITHFUL and the husband only put her away -- but did not give her a certificate of divorce -- should she marry someone else (like they could in that culture), the husband was held responsible before God. He caused her second marriage to be considered adulterous in God's opinion. He was as guilty for the adultery as she was. Why? He didn't legally divorce her. He was still legally married to her. Because he already had put her away, he should have legally divorced her so she would be free from her first marriage before getting into another relationship. God is holding him responsible for not giving the divorce.

The second point Jesus was making by adding the exception had to do with IF THE WOMAN WAS UNFAITHFUL. In that case: if the man's spouse had sex with someone else -- or ever married someone else after having been sexually unfaithful in the marriage -- the husband, who put her away is not responsible for their spouse's future life and decisions. He wasn't responsible for her adultery. It was acceptable to just put her away. He is not responsible for the things she may do, nor is he causing her to commit adultery with a future spouse. Why? Adultery had already been committed. The covenant was broken. He could put her away and move on to a future relationship without giving her a certificate of divorce. In a situation of unfaithfulness, he did not need to give her a divorce to be clean before God.

Surprise, surprise -- Jesus is actually making a case for the need to get a legal divorce and end the broken marriage correctly. He's not arguing against divorce. Jesus is emphasizing that if one partner is going to put the other way, they need to make it a legitimate legal divorce and be done with the marriage relationship, and in that way prevent an additional adultery situation.

> *Jesus is actually making a case for the need to get a legal divorce and end the broken marriage correctly.*

Nowhere in this section of scripture does Jesus say He's against a legal divorce. In fact, He's agreeing with the Old Testament Law and saying the opposite. He's saying there is a time to get the divorce.

Let's make sure we are seeing this as it applies to our culture and time. To apply it to our time, there are only two details that need to be emphasized:

1.) We are not allowed to simply put someone away without giving them a legal divorce. It's illegal for them to remarry under those circumstances. In our culture, if a marriage dissolves, we need to make it legal at the courthouse.

2.) In our culture, the man can put away and divorce the woman, and she can do the same to the man. Either one can initiate. It's not just a one-sided process like it was in Jesus' time. (Jesus must have known that was coming, because He says it in Mark 10:11-12.)

Other than those two points, everything else applies today. Jesus is agreeing with the Old Testament that it's the "putting away" that is wrong and is sin. That is what breaks the covenant. Once the covenant has been broken, Jesus says it needs to be finished the right way, and the paperwork needs to be taken care of. In other words, get a legal certificate or writing of divorce.

I could say many things here about why this is Godly and just. But I will save them for chapter 8, in which I make the summary and application.

Let's look at another scripture.

Mt 19:3-9 (NIV - underline and bracketed Greek words added)
Some Pharisees came to him to test him. They asked, "Is it lawful for a man to divorce ["apoluo" – "put away"] his wife for any and every reason?" "Haven't you read," he replied, "that at the beginning the Creator 'made them male and female,' and said, 'For this reason a man will leave his father and mother and be united to his wife, and the two will become one flesh'? So they are no longer two, but one. Therefore what God has joined together, let man not separate." "Why then," they asked, "did Moses command that a man give his wife a certificate of divorce ["apostasion"] and send her away ["apoluo"]?" Jesus replied, "Moses permitted you to divorce ["apoluo" – "put away"] your wives because your hearts were hard. But it was not this way from

the beginning. I tell you that anyone who <u>divorces</u> ["apoluo" – "puts away"] his wife, except for marital unfaithfulness, and marries another woman commits adultery."

Again here the KJV does a much better job of translation. The correct distinction is definitely made between a writing of divorcement, and putting away.

Mt 19:3-9 (KJV - underline added)
[3] The Pharisees also came unto him, tempting him, and saying unto him, "Is it lawful for a man to <u>put away</u> his wife for every cause"? [4] And he answered and said unto them, "Have ye not read, that he which made them at the beginning made them male and female, [5] And said, For this cause shall a man leave father and mother, and shall cleave to his wife: and they twain shall be one flesh? [6] Wherefore they are no more twain, but one flesh. What therefore God hath joined together, let not man put asunder." [7] They say unto him, "Why did Moses then command to give a <u>writing of divorcement</u>, and to <u>put her away</u>?" [8] He saith unto them, "Moses because of the hardness of your hearts suffered you to <u>put away</u> your wives: but from the beginning it was not so. [9] And I say unto you, Whosoever shall <u>put away his wife</u>, except it be for fornication, and shall marry another, committeth adultery: and whoso marrieth her which is <u>put away</u> doth commit adultery."

This section of scripture has quite a bit more information than the previous one we looked at. So let's take this apart and see what Jesus is saying.

One thing I'd like to point out is that in this scripture, Jesus never directly addresses the writing of divorcement. All His answers have to do with putting away. That is important, because Jesus is going to address the core of what's wrong in a broken covenant and give God's input on it. He's not even touching the paperwork aspect -- the part most people today would call getting a divorce.

Here, we have a test being laid out for Jesus, and it has to do with divorce and remarriage. They knew the difference between putting away and a writing of divorcement. So they are trying to trap Jesus. In reality, they probably didn't really want to know the answer to the question they asked, because it says their true motivation for asking was to "test" or "tempt" Him. However, they did ask a question that Jesus did answer. So no matter their motives, it does give us some insight into how Jesus viewed putting away, divorce, and remarriage.

Their first question was whether it was right (according to the law of Moses) to put away a woman, "for any and every reason" (NIV) or "every cause" (KJV). They are really asking a generalized question. Another way of saying it would be: can we put away our wives whenever we want to?

Jesus answers that question by going back to the original design for marriage. He quotes Genesis 1:27 and 2:24 and says two things that probably shocked them.

> 1.) This is not a matter of just getting rid of someone in your life. There has been a spiritual and emotional joining -- "cleave to his wife" (KJV), "united to his wife" (NIV) -- as well as a physical joining during the sexual aspect of the marriage -- "they twain shall be one flesh" (KJV), "and the two will be come one flesh" (NIV). The result is, "they are no longer two, but one" (NIV) which is the concept of covenant. Jesus was saying that to put someone away is to take a new living entity that had been formed when they were married (the new "one") and ripping it apart.

This agrees with what what many translations say in Malachi 2:15 -- that there is a "remnant" or "residue" of the spirit that remains.

(Malachi 2:15 (KJV - underline added)
[15] And did not he make one? <u>Yet had he the residue of the spirit.</u> And wherefore one? That he might seek a Godly seed. Therefore take heed to your spirit, and let none deal treacherously against the wife of his youth.

If you take the time to look at it in many different translations, from time to time there will be a footnote at the end of this phrase that says something like, "the actual meaning is uncertain." So in other words, the Hebrew word here in Malachi is difficult to translate, and they're not sure they're getting it right.

It seems to indicate that when a couple is married, a new spirit is formed between the two. This would make perfect sense, because the two are no longer who they used to be, but are united as "one" new identity. This is covenant language. God is saying that when someone is put away, that spiritual forming and entity is destroyed, and He's left with a spiritual "residue" or "remnant." What is He to do with it? It's another reason He hates putting away (v. 16).

2.) Then He said something more shocking: "therefore what God has joined together, let man not separate" (NIV), "what therefore God hath joined together, let not *man* put asunder" (KJV).

Now stop and think about this: who was asking Him the question? The Pharisees. They were *men*. In essence, Jesus is telling them as *men*, they have no right to put their wives away for any and every reason (which was the question they asked).

I want to make sure we don't miss a very important point here. Jesus is clearly stating that God's perspective on marriage is that no one should ever be put away (v. 4-6). He states it later in the passage, but God's opinion on a covenant being broken and a marriage failing has to do with one thing: the hardness of the people's hearts. If we go back to the original design, God is opposed to a spouse ever being put away and the marriage ending in divorce.

So in answering their question: can a wife be put away for "any and every reason or cause? Jesus said, no; it isn't right. Then He gives the explanation of the original design for marriage.

The Pharisees had their first question answered, but now they have another question (v. 7). Their question was this: if it's wrong to put away a wife for every cause, why did the law of Moses command they should "give her a writing of divorcement" and "put her away" (KJV)? Jesus' answer: they were allowed to put her away because their hearts were so hard.

There are two things we need to notice in Jesus' answer:

> 1.) Jesus does not contradict the law of Moses. He gives explanation as to why God commanded what He did.

> 2.) Jesus did not say they were given the right to give a *writing of divorcement* because their hearts were hard. He specifically said they were allowed to *put away* the spouse because their hearts were hard.

You may say, "What's the point?" The point is this: Jesus isn't concerned about the writing of divorcement. It isn't the issue. The problem of the broken covenant and marriage wasn't with the paperwork. He went to the source of the problem -- the hard hearts which caused the putting away.

The major point Jesus was emphasizing in this discussion had to do with having a *hard heart*. What does it mean to have a hard heart? When we search through what Jesus had to say about hard-hearted people, there is one thing in common among the verses: it has to do with failing to understand "spiritual" things. That is what He's saying here. The reason they were given the right to put away their wives and give them a writing of divorcement was because they didn't comprehend the spiritual side of marriage. He goes on to say that from the beginning (original creation), it wasn't set up to work that way. The position Jesus took here still applies today. The lack of spiritual understanding due to hardness of heart is *a* -- if not *the* -- basic reason for so many divorces today.

He said that any man who puts away his wife -- for any reason except one "marital unfaithfulness" (NIV) or "fornication" (KJV) by the wife -- and then marries again or remarries, is committing adultery (please notice: He said "puts away", not "divorces"). This point was explained in Matthew 5, the passage that we previously looked at. But Jesus adds a few pieces of new information here, so I'll deal with it again.

> *The lack of spiritual understanding due to hardness of heart is "a" -- if not "the" -- basic reason for so many divorces today.*

Why would He make an exception to the rule? In God's mind, the wife had been unfaithful to the husband. The covenant was already broken by her unfaithfulness. Therefore, putting her away without giving her a certificate of divorce was acceptable, just like in Matthew 5. The wife broke the covenant. The husband was innocent in this, so like we saw in the explanation of Matthew 5, the husband was spared a lot of unfair problems by being allowed to simply put her away and not give her the writing of divorce. Also, He wouldn't be held guilty of causing adultery, because it had already been committed.

Now Jesus' adds a facet to the process that He didn't talk about in Matthew 5. When dealing with a situation where there HAS NOT been sexual unfaithfulness, He says if the husband does not legally divorce his wife (writing of divorcement), and HE marries another woman -- then HE'S in adultery also. That's different than in Matthew 5. There it said only SHE AND HER NEW SPOUSE were in adultery. Why would HE be in adultery also (v. 9)? Because he's also still legally married to the first wife, and has sinned against her by putting her away without giving her a legal divorce. So when he remarries, God is still holding him accountable to the first covenant he made with the first wife. They haven't divorced. They're still married.

> *Every situation where a putting away had occurred, a writing of divorce (legal divorce) also had to be given.*

Every situation in which a putting away had occurred, a writing of divorce (legal divorce) also had to be given. Again, Jesus was addressing situations where unfaithfulness HAD NOT taken place (like in Matthew 5:31-32). When one was put away, a legal divorce had to be given; otherwise if they ever married again, both of them would be in adultery.

Let's touch the "white elephant" question that's in many minds right now. If a husband *does* legally divorce his wife, can he get remarried? According to Jesus -- yes. In the context of this scripture, Jesus was explaining the necessity of getting the divorce if unfaithfulness HAD NOT HAPPENED. Once someone was divorced, they could remarry without being in adultery, because they were no longer married to the first spouse.

Again, like we saw in Matthew 5:31-32, there is only one exception that gave the husband the right to *put her away and NOT give the legal divorce.* It had to do with the wife HAVING BEEN INVOLVED in "fornication" or "sexual unfaithfulness". If this had taken place, the husband didn't have to divorce his wife, he could just move on and get remarried.

In either situation -- whether unfaithfulness HAD or HAD NOT oc-curred -- he was free to remarry.

Let's look at the situation involving fornication. What is Jesus really talking about when he refers to fornication?

The word for fornication in the Greek is, "porneia". It has two basic meanings:

The first basic meaning is any form of unlawful sex.

In the scriptural context, that refers to the law of Moses under which they were living at the time. "Porneia" or "fornication" is a general term that refers to any type of sexual activity with someone or some-thing that is outside of a marriage covenant. Interestingly, pornography can also fall in under fornication. The word pornography comes from the Greek word "pornographos", which means to write about sexual activity or having sex with prostitutes. At this time in history, pornog-raphy was not in picture or video format so the sexual act could be seen; pictures and videos are only a fairly recent advent. Instead, it was written about. Notice: the first four letters of the word

191

*porn*ography were actually kept from the Greek words from which it was derived: *porn*ographos and *porn*eia. It's also the abbreviated form of the word we use to refer to pornography: we call it "porn".

What's the point? When Jesus was talking about fornication, He wasn't only talking about physical sex; He was also talking about pornography.

> The second basic meaning of "porneia" in this verse is idolatry.

Idolatry is speaking of two possible things:

> 1.) the worship of an idol or,
>
> 2.) a strong or excessive love, admiration, fondness, or reverence for something or someone.

That really makes no sense in the context of marriage unless you understand the concept of covenant. Remember, when we are in a marriage covenant with someone, they are to be put first in our lives above anyone and anything else except God. This definition of idolatry says that when someone or something is placed above our spouse in importance, we are in fornication. That's why God used the word "porneia" when He referred to spiritual fornication or adultery, which was spiritually placing someone or something above God in importance (Revelation 17:2, 17:4, 18:3, 19:2).

This second meaning of "porneia" is much different than simply having sex outside of marriage. It's talking about something that God considers a form of idolatry. This second concept of fornication includes basically anything in which we get involved that places our spouse second to someone or something else. Wow! That's really intense. Paul deals with this concept in 1 Corinthians 7 when he talks about marriage. We will look at that scripture a little later.

I want to address something again so I can point out where many Christians have been misled and why. This scripture has also been used to say that if a person is divorced and remarries, they are in adultery. It is not saying that. We've already shown what it is really saying if you put the correct Greek words into the passage and not the mis-translated verbiage. A few translations have it right, but most do not. Out of the 57 versions of the Bible that I checked, only 14 translated this verse correctly, using put away and not divorce. Here are the 14 that I found to be correct: 21st Century KJV, Confraternity Version, ASV, BRG, Darby, DLNT, DRA, JUB, KJV, AKJV, OJB, WE, WYC, and YLT. I'm not sure why so many translators got it wrong. I've researched many different theories, which range from a preference in personal beliefs of the translators to church or denomination loyalties. The fact remains: too many have translated it incorrectly. I checked Protestant Bibles, Catholic Bibles, and Jewish Bibles. All faiths had some versions that were correct, and they also had incorrect versions.

I want it clearly understood that there seem to be two things that have caused the confusion and misunderstandings:

1.) The translation inaccuracies probably play the biggest role in the problem. When people read different translations, and the translations use "divorce" instead of "put away", the reader accepts "divorce" as the right word. As a result, they believe it's the word divorce as we would understand divorce in our culture today. That misunderstanding is then applied to the verbiage of our culture, and they come up with the idea that if someone gets a divorce and marries again, they are in adultery, which is incorrect.

2.) Again because of translation incongruities, most people have come to the conclusion that "putting away" and "divorce" mean the same thing. When comparing translations, they are used interchangeably. Therefore the reader concludes they are describing the same thing: it's talking about when a person gets a divorce. Again, this creates a problem, because it's not correct.

The point I want to be sure we take away from v. 9 is that Jesus did not say if a divorced person remarries, they are in adultery. He said that if a person is only put away, but not legally divorced, and either one re-marry without getting the legal divorce, they are both in adultery in the second marriage.

Please notice this: Jesus emphasized "putting away" -- not "divorce." He used some form of the word "put away" five different times in Matthew 19:3-9. Jesus never said the word "divorce" (the writing or bill of divorcement) once in this passage of scripture. The Pharisees brought it up, and He answered their question about it, but Jesus never repeated the word used for divorce. He focused on the putting away aspect of the process.

> *Jesus is emphasizing "putting away" -- not "divorce."*

What does that tell us? That Jesus, speaking for God and being an exact representation of the Father (Hebrews 1:3 -- NIV), is not focused on the paperwork of divorce. He's looking at what actually broke the covenant and led to the courtroom and paperwork (bill of divorce). That means it is also the Father's position. From God's perspective, the legal paperwork is not the issue. It is simply the result of someone having been "put away" and the covenant being broken.

Once the covenant is broken, there needs to be reconciliation or a legal divorce so the other person can go on with their life without living in adultery.

In America, our government requires the legal portion of the process. We can't be legally married to two different people at the same time. But remember, in the culture of Jesus' day, polygamy was an accepted practice. When Jesus answered this question, He wasn't coming from a Western mindset.

Simply put, putting away is the result of a bad marriage. It is when a person (man or woman -- Mark 10:11-12) is dismissed or released from the bond and union that is to happen in marriage. What the marriage was intended to be was allowed to die. One spouse put the other away. This destroys the original design for marriage. Since the marriage is dead, one partner files for a divorce. It's not necessarily the fault of the person who actually files the paperwork for the divorce (this was shown in reference to God divorcing Israel in Jeremiah 3).

They are putting an end to something that is already dead. It's not to be assumed that it was their fault that the marriage is dead. I heard a man talking about this, and he compared it to signing a death certificate. The person is dead. Is the person who identifies the fact that they're dead at fault? Is he now the reason the other person died, just because he signed and filed the death certificate? Of course not. The person was already dead. The same is true about filing the legal paperwork for a divorce.

> *Divorce is simply the result of someone having been "put away" and the covenant being broken.*

However, the putting away or letting the marriage die typically happens while the couple is still living together. Someone (or both) lives their life independently of their spouse. Often they do this in a devaluing and even abusive manner. This can be done spiritually, emotionally, mentally, and physically. It can be one area at a time, but most likely it is a combination of areas. No matter how it's done, it falls under putting away.

It happens all the time in marriages. The two people may even stay physically living together, but they have "put" the other person "out" of their life. They don't like the other person or may even hate them. As a result, they live separate lives while living together. They each have their own friends, checkbooks, financial situations, hobbies, recreations, cars, etc. They sleep in separate beds. They live in different parts of the house. Much of the time, the only thing they may do together is eat a meal, possibly go to church or some holiday gathering with the relatives, and file their taxes -- "jointly". One of the partners has been "put out of" or "put away" from the life of the other (or they've both put each other away). But they haven't filed the legal paperwork that would declare them divorced. They still live under that same roof; so in society's, the relatives', and often the church's eyes, the couple is still married. In God's eyes, they are very likely in a broken covenant or marriage situation, and He no longer considers them married.

The Baby Boomer generation saw a lot of this type of putting away in their parents and grand-parents, and as a result -- in their generation -- divorce sky-rocketed. They were not going to live like their parents! According to what Jesus said, they were right. They shouldn't live in a relationship like that.

The scary part is that in the Old Testament and in Jesus' time, this thing was even worse. Because polygamy was an accepted practice, it was common for a man to literally put away a wife he didn't like. History records that sometimes the woman still lived in the house with the other wives, and sometimes she was literally driven out to live alone. An example of being driven out to live alone happened with Abraham with Hagar. However, since she was never given a bill of divorce, she could not remarry. The result was that she was forced into a life of solitude (e.g. Tamar in II Samuel 13:11-20) or adultery by way of remarriage, or living with someone to whom she wasn't married. What caused Abraham to do that? Sarah, his first wife.

Now, I know that some will say that Hagar wasn't Abraham's wife, but only Sarah's servant who bore a child for Abraham (like a concubine). But that is incorrect. Most translations agree that she became his wife.

Genesis 16:3 (NIV)
[3] So after Abram had been living in Canaan ten years, Sarai his wife took her Egyptian maidservant Hagar and gave her to her husband to be his wife.

Why did this unfortunate event take place? Because of Sarah's unbelief. There is no indication it was ever God's idea for Abraham to have a child through Hagar, but it happened. Abraham took a second wife. There were problems between the women, and Abraham gave Sarah permission to do with Hagar whatever she wanted. As a result, Hagar was treated so badly that she left. What was actually happening here? Abraham and Sarah had put Hagar away and was literally sent away by Abraham when he said, "Do with her whatever you think is best" (Genesis 16:6). He wasn't protecting her or doing what a husband should do to keep a marriage intact. Abraham broke the marriage covenant with her.

Anyone looking in can see that this is wrong. We know that God was watching, because who came to Hagar's rescue? God. And who defended her by giving her the promise of a huge number of offspring? God. It's stated as, "the Angel of the Lord" came to her (v. 7, 9, 11). Most commentators believe that when the Old Testament refers to "the Angel of the Lord", it is referring to a pre-incarnate appearance or visitation from Jesus. If that is correct, it was actually Jesus who came and took care of, defended, and blessed Hagar. Right from the beginning, God hated the concept of mistreating a woman and putting her away. As in Hagar's case, it had to do with abuse and abandonment. This is another example of what God said in Malachi 2:16 -- He hates it when a wife is put away and violated.

We know it was God who intervened on Hagar's behalf, whether it was an angel or actually a pre-incarnate Jesus who came to her. She also knew it was God. In v. 13, Hagar said this:

Genesis 16:13-14 (NIV – bracketed words added)
[13] She gave this name to the LORD who spoke to her: "You are the God who sees me," for she said, "I have now seen [Or seen the back of] the One who sees me." [14] That is why the well was called Beer Lahai Roi [Beer Lahai Roi means well of the Living One who sees me.]; [Ge 24:62; 25:11] it is still there, between Kadesh and Bered.

Now let's get back to the main thought:

The right to simply put away a spouse, especially if polygamy was involved, was a ready-made tool to maintain control of your wife. It was always hanging over her head that if she didn't do what the man wanted, she could be put away. Of course, polygamy didn't affect the man negatively, because he would just marry more wives. However, it was not acceptable for a woman to have more than one husband. If she was put away, she had to stay alone, but the man could marry as many wives as he wanted. He wasn't concerned about being alone. It was the epideme of a Chauvinistic society.

God was furious with this practice! It was totally against the original purpose for marriage.It also completely violated and devalued the woman.

I need to make a point here: from what I can see in scripture, the way God looks at divorce and remarriage has not changed between the Old and New Testaments. Jesus did not state that there was any change necessary in the area of divorce and remarriage from the Law of Moses. In fact, aside from the various Old Testament Laws, Jesus upheld the basic premise of what was said in the Old Testament about divorce and remarriage. Paul confirms the same principles in his writings. The apostles didn't say anything had changed in their writings either. Again, I state: aside from the various Old Testament Laws regarding putting away, divorce, and remarriage, neither Paul nor any of the other writers of the New Testament stated any change from the Old Testament in how the basic concepts of marriage, divorce, and remarriage were to be handled.

Please notice that the adultery issue is connected to remarriage only when someone has been put away and not legally divorced.

When the Pharisees approached Jesus on Divorce, they had asked if it was all right to dismiss the wife for "any and every cause". This had become the practice by Christ's time. They would literally get rid of the spouse for any reason.

Here is how Luke relates not only what Jesus said about putting away, but also how Jesus felt about it.

Luke 16:16-18 (KJV - underline added)
[16] The law and the prophets were until John: since that time the kingdom of God is preached, and every man presseth into it. [17] And it is easier for heaven and earth to pass, than one tittle of the law to fail. [18] Whosoever <u>putteth away</u> his wife, and marrieth another, committeth adultery: and whosoever marrieth her that is <u>put away</u> from her husband committeth adultery.

Notice the order in which he put this: He's explaining and dealing with the Old Testament Law again and how the switch was going toward emphasizing the Kingdom of God. However, even in that new emphasis, nothing in the law will be lost or pass away. Then He gives an example: if you put away your wife and marry another, you are committing adultery; and the person marrying her who is put away will also be in adultery.

In the verses in Matthew 5 & 19 that we've already looked at, Jesus included an exception which had to do with fornication or adultery. In Luke 16, Jesus did not include that exception. This is why when I was dealing with the passages in Matthew 5 & 19, I said Jesus was dealing with two separate scenarios. One was without the exception, and one was with the exception. This passage in Luke 16 proves that point. Here Jesus leaves out the exception. He is just dealing with putting away and remarriage when there HAS NOT been any marital unfaithfulness.

Please notice that the adultery issue is connected to remarriage only when someone has been put away and not legally divorced. This is the point I was making in Matthew 5. I point it out here because it is easier to see it in these verses.

Otherwise, Luke 16 agrees with everything we've seen to this point, so let's look at Mark 10:2-12.

Mark 10 is very close to the Matthew 19 passage, so I won't re-explain all the things that were already touched when we looked at Matthew 19. However, some additions are found in v. 3-4 and v. 11-12. Again I'll use the KJV, because it is more accurate in differentiating between putting away and divorce.

Mark 10:2-12 (KJV - underline added)
[2] And the Pharisees came to him, and asked him, "Is it lawful for a man to put away his wife?" tempting him. [3] And he answered and said unto them, "What did Moses command you?" [4] And they said, Moses suffered to write a bill of divorcement, and to put her away [5] And Jesus answered and said unto them, "For the hardness of your heart he wrote you this precept. [6] But from the beginning of the creation God made them male and female. [7] For this cause shall a man leave his father and mother, and cleave to his wife; [8] And they twain shall be one flesh: so then they are no more twain, but one flesh. [9] What therefore God hath joined together, let not man put asunder." [10] And in the house his disciples asked him again of the same matter. [11] And he saith unto them, "Whosoever shall put away his wife, and marry another, committeth adultery against her. [12] And if a woman shall put away her husband, and be married to another, she committeth adultery."

There are three points we need to see here.

1.) When putting a spouse away, we are commanded to give the bill of divorcement.

2.) Jesus makes it plain that the same principle of putting away applies to both men and women. It is adultery both ways.

201

3.) Again, Jesus is dealing with the subject without the exception of sexual unfaithfulness.

Let's look at these:

1.) In v. 2, the Pharisees asked Jesus if it's lawful to put away a man's wife. Jesus asked what Moses commanded. They said, if a man puts a woman away, "Moses *suffered* to give her a bill of divorcement." The word "suffered" comes from two Greek words meaning to superimpose something and to turn. The bill of divorcement is to be "superimposed" onto the process and "turned" over to the one who is put away. In other words, the legal paperwork is to be part of, or attached to, the putting away. Once a spouse is put away, it is *commanded* (v. 3) that the legal paperwork be included in the process. Both elements need to be done together so they will be legally divorced. Jesus confirmed that was correct, stating the reason Moses commanded and suffered them to do it that way.

So, if a spouse has been put away, it's a *command* that they be given a bill of divorce (legally divorced). That point is very important. Why? Because God is putting His stamp of approval on the "legal divorce" aspect of the process. God is saying that if, in an unfortunate situation, someone is put away in a marriage, you are commanded to carry through on the paper work also. Technically speaking, God is in favor of the "divorce" aspect of the process. He's "for" giving the certificate of divorce.

But remember, He's never in favor of the putting away aspect of the process.

2.) In v. 11-12, Jesus states that both men and women can initiate the "putting away" of their spouse.

This is very important for our cultural time, because now it can happen either way. The husband can put away and divorce his wife, or the wife can put away and divorce her husband. It was good that Mark added another aspect of what Jesus had said. It makes it very relevant to our culture.

3.) I'd like to point out something else in v. 11-12: Jesus doesn't mention whether there was a legitimate reason to put the other away or not. He did not use the exception clause of fornication or adultery. He is simply stating it as a fact that putting away had happened (v. 11-12).

The stated purpose for doing this was in order to marry another woman (v. 11-12). This would leave the current spouse (particularly the wife) either begging to be taken in by a relative, a slave in her own household, or possibly homeless and on the street. There was no government program or federal helps for her in that culture. To survive, she often resorted to living with another man or marrying another man. This, of course, was adultery, since her first husband did not give her a bill of divorce.

In our mindset, we might assume the government would catch the fact that he or she was already married to another person before issuing another marriage license. Today, that would likely happen. But remember, back in that time the government was not the one keeping the records. The parents of the couple would keep the written marriage agreements - - presuming there were any. From my research, it seemed that in many cases there were no written marriage agreements in place at all. The only thing that was kept as proof of the agreement was typically the token of virginity (the cloth that contained the blood of the woman from the wedding night that proved she was a virgin when they consummated the marriage). Her parents kept this in the event that an accusation concerning her virginity would come up in the future. Other than that, there were no county or state records to verify that a wedding had ever taken place.

What I'm about to explain to you now is one of the reasons we now have county, state, and even federal records of a marriage. It's a good thing our forefathers had the wisdom to put those laws into place. Records are needed to prevent what was happening then -- and would still be happening now -- if it weren't for the paper trail

> *Technically speaking, God is in favor of the "divorce" aspect of the process.*
>
> *But remember, He's never in favor of the "putting away" aspect of the process.*

that follows a marriage. People would still be doing what they were doing back then. Instead of going through the hassle and expense of legally separating, they would just leave one spouse and go to another.

Back in Jesus' time, polygamy was easy. If they stayed in a small community where everyone knew each other, this didn't work well. However, if they simply relocated to an area where they were not known, they could easily remarry, and no one would ever find out they were still married to someone else. There was no real way to track them. There were no social security numbers, no driver's license numbers, no medical records, no dental records -- there was no way to track a person.

So what did they do? Exactly what I described. This was especially true in a woman's situation, where she likely had no job skills or employment outside the home. What was she going to do to survive? She would simply remarry. That's what Jesus was addressing. It was wrong to put a woman or a man in the situation where they were abandoned or simply thrown out -- especially for women in that culture, since they had no way to survive unless someone in their family took them in or they found another husband. As a result, many ended up in adultery. It was a sin against the woman and the very purpose a marriage had been formed. That's what made God angry and what He wanted to stop.

Next let's look at Romans 7.

Romans 7:1-4 (NIV - underline added)
[1] Do you not know, brothers—for I am speaking to men who know the law—that the law has authority over a man only as long as he lives? [2] For example, by law a married woman is <u>bound</u> to her husband as long as he is alive, but if her husband dies, she is <u>released</u> from the law of marriage. [3] So then, if she marries another man while her husband is still alive, she is called an adulteress. But if her husband dies, she is <u>released</u> from that law and is not an adulteress, even though she marries another man. [4] So, my brothers, you also died to the law through the body of Christ, that you might belong to another, to him who was raised from the dead, in order that we might bear fruit to God.

To understand this scripture more easily, we need to put it into the context of the rest of the Bible. We've seen that when a written divorce was not given -- but there was only a putting away -- should either partner remarry, they were in adultery. However, if a bill of divorcement had been given, then remarriage for either partner was not considered adultery. Since the marriage had been dissolved through a written divorce, the persons involved were no longer married. The term "adultery" didn't apply in the situation.

In Romans 7, Paul is using the picture of marriage as an example. Divorce, putting away and remarriage are not his point. That's why he doesn't use those terms in this section of scripture.

Paul's point was to show the Roman people how the Law stayed in effect in their lives until there was a death. Since they had died to the Law in Christ, the Old Testament Law no longer had any power over them.

Then he used marriage as an example of the wife being released from the Law when the husband dies. Once she is "released" (no longer "bound"), she is free to marry another man.

The point and application was: they had died in Christ, so they were free from the Law, and now could belong to (marry) Jesus. This also agrees with the picture of marriage between the church and Jesus of which Paul speaks in Ephesians 5:22-33.

By using marriage and adultery as an example, Paul is clearly addressing the common practice of adultery as it pertained to the Old Testament Law (v. 1 -- "for I am speaking to men who know the law"). His point in referencing the law was that unless a writing of divorce was given, remarrying after putting away one's spouse was considered adultery. They weren't "released" to remarry without the paperwork. This is what it said in the Law, and if there's anyone who knew the Law, it was Paul. They were still "bound" to that person in marriage as long as that person was alive.

These verses in Romans 7 have nothing to do with the belief that says a person cannot get a divorce and then remarry, and if they do, they're in adultery.

Just like in the Old Testament, Paul is addressing the issue of getting remarried without having been released. If you remember, the Law said the person had to be given a certificate or "bill of divorcement" to be released from the marriage; they could not have only been put away. If the woman had not been divorced, according to the Law, she was still married and could not marry another. If she did, she was in adultery as long as her husband was alive (because legally, she's still married or "bound" to him). Once he dies, she is no longer "bound" to her husband. That word "bound" is important. We are going to discuss it in connection with 1 Corinthians 7 a little later.

Romans 7 has nothing to do with the church's traditional belief that says if a person is divorced and remarried, they are living in adultery.

According to the Law, there were only 2 ways of being released from or no longer "bound" to the husband. (1.) He had to die (Romans 7:1-4), or (2.) she had to be given a written certificate of divorce (stated in the Old Testament Law - cf. Deuteronomy 24:1-4). That is Paul's whole point here and it's why he used marriage as an example.

His point is that our death in Christ releases us from the Old Testament Law the same way the death of a spouse releases them from their marriage.

This goes along with what we said about Tamar and Amnon. What Paul laid out here as the Law is likely part of the reason Absalom killed Amnon. They couldn't bring the rape out into the open, because they were relatives, and both Amnon and Tamar may be killed. But the problem could be resolved, and Tamar would be released from Amnon if he was dead. And that's exactly what happened. Amnon ended up dead, and his death "released' Tamar from the marriage. She was no longer "bound" to him because of death.

This passage in Romans 7 has nothing to do with the church's traditional belief that says if a person is divorced and remarried, they are living in adultery. That was not Paul's point, and he doesn't say that. He says if the spouse is still alive (and you haven't been released from the marriage -- obviously by divorce), and you remarry someone else -- you are in adultery. Why? For the same reasons we've seen to this point: you are still married. Once the person is released from the marriage (and Paul only refers to one of the ways of being released in Romans 7 which was death, because it fits better to illustrate his point), from the marriage -- they can remarry and not be in adultery.

> Paul only applied being "bound" to a spouse and "released" from them in the case of a death in Romans 7. But in 1 Corinthians 7, he will apply it to divorce also.

So let's look at 1 Corinthians 7:10-16. The entire chapter deals with marriage issues. We're going to look primarily at the portion of this chapter that deals with the divorce issue. Paul states his general position on the subject in v. 10-11.

I'm going to give the NIV version first, so you can see how it is mistranslated.

1 Corinthians 7:10-11 (NIV - underline added)
[10] To the married I give this command (not I, but the Lord): A wife must not separate from her husband. [11] But if she does, she must re-main unmarried or else be reconciled to her husband. And a husband must not <u>divorce</u> his wife.

Again, the NIV mistranslates the end of verse 11. The KJV is more accurate.

1 Corinthians 7:10-11 (KJV - underline added)
[10] And unto the married I command, yet not I, but the Lord, Let not

the wife depart from her husband: [11] But and if she depart, let her remain unmarried, or be reconciled to her husband: and let not the husband put away his wife.

The first thing I'd like to point out is that Paul is talking to the "married" (v. 10), not the unmarried.

In verse 10 it says the wife must "not separate" (NIV), "let not the wife depart" (KJV) from her husband. The Greek word here ("chorizo") carries the same connotation as putting away. It is talking about separating away from a person. In essence, Paul is saying that a wife shouldn't put her husband away or separate from him. If she does, she needs to remain unmarried.

In verse 11, it says the husband should not put away his wife. Notice the difference. NIV says "divorce", whereas the KJV says "put away." Again, *put away* is the correct translation.

Paul isn't talking about a written paper or certificate of divorce. He's talking about what happened in the marriage -- the putting away aspect -- that eventually causes a divorce (as we've already found in other scriptures). He is also showing the fact that it can go both directions: the man can put away the woman, and the woman can put away the man. Paul is stating what the Lord feels about it. He wants people to remain married. By stating they must remain unmarried, the Lord -- through Paul -- is also reaffirming that if the only thing they do is put each other away, they need to remain unmarried. Why? We already know the answer to that question: to remarry without the divorce paperwork would put both of them into adultery.

In the next verses, he addresses an area where putting away is acceptable, which should end in a legal divorce.

1 Corinthians 7:12 (NIV - underline added)
[12] To the rest I say this (I, not the Lord): If any brother has a wife who is not a believer and she is willing to live with him, he must not <u>divorce</u> her.

Notice: the NIV uses the word "divorce" again. That is another instance of an incorrect translation. It should be "put away." Again, the KJV is more accurate on this. So, let's use the KJV.

1 Corinthians 7:12-16 (KJV - underline added)
[12] But to the rest speak I, not the Lord: If any brother hath a wife that believeth not, and she be pleased to dwell with him, let him not <u>put her away</u>. [13] And the woman which hath an husband that believeth not, and if he be pleased to dwell with her, <u>let her not leave him</u>. [14] For the unbelieving husband is sanctified by the wife, and the unbelieving wife is sanctified by the husband: else were your children unclean; but now are they holy. [15] But if the unbelieving depart, let him depart. A brother or a sister is not <u>under bondage</u> in such cases: but God hath called us to peace. [16] For what knowest thou, O wife, whether thou shalt save thy husband? or how knowest thou, O man, whether thou shalt save thy wife?

Paul begins by saying, "To the rest speak I." In verse 10, he said he was speaking to married people only. Now, for the rest of the chapter, he's including the married as well as those who are not married.

The next thing he says is, "Speak I, not the Lord." He's stating that he doesn't have a direct word from the Lord on what he's about to say, but he's going to give it his best effort to answer their questions with answers that he thinks Jesus would give. He also re-states that same thing in v. 25 and v. 40. In other words, from v. 12-40 of chapter 7, Paul is speaking from what he knows and is giving the best advice he can from what he knows the Lord is like and wants.

So what is Paul talking about here? The context would obviously be dealing with what, in our culture, we would call divorce. However, Paul doesn't use the word "apostasion", which would refer to a written divorce paper. He uses a different word: "aphiemi", which is also defined as sending or putting away. Paul's primary focus in this section of scripture is not the paperwork or certificate of divorce that one would get in court. He's talking about putting away a spouse. Technically, Paul is NOT adding another reason for divorce. When an unbelieving spouse leaves the believer, they are in essence putting the believer "away" or "out" of their life. The same principles that we've seen on putting away, divorce, and remarriage still apply.

Now, I realize that if we put a spouse away, the process must carry through so it ends in what we call a divorce. Otherwise, as we already discovered, it becomes an injustice to the one who is only put away but not given a certificate of divorce. That's the whole point Paul is making here -- don't put the other person away, or simply walk away. The reason Paul gives for putting away or "leaving him" is this: they don't agree with your beliefs in God (v. 12). In v. 13 he reiterates the same thing, just in the reverse order (again I point out that it's good that it was written this way. It applies more directly to our culture where either partner can initiate a divorce). In my words, this is Paul's point in v. 12-13:

Just because you have a mixed marriage -- where one person believes in and is serving God and the other doesn't -- is not a reason to put them away. As long as the unbeliever is willing or pleased to stay with you -- in spite of the fact that you are serving God -- you shouldn't look for a way out of the marriage. Stay married.

Every divorce begins with one spouse putting the other away. If we never put them away, there will never be a divorce. It's back to the same subject that we have been seeing throughout the scripture. God is upset when one spouse puts away the other spouse. That's what breaks the covenant. God doesn't want that happening. Paul echoes that sentiment here in this chapter.

Let's look a little more at the "willing" or "pleased" point he is making in this passage. In v. 12, Paul says that if we are in this situation where a man is married to a woman who is not a believer and *she is willing or pleased to live with him even though he is a believer*, he should not put her away because she isn't a believer. In v. 13, it's the same point, the only difference being that the woman should not leave the man.

Do you remember the reason Paul would say it that way -- "let her not leave him?" It's because in the culture of that time, women had no rights. A woman could not initiate a divorce. The only thing she could do was leave. With that in mind, it's easy to see that Paul is talking about the same thing with both the man and the woman: don't put your spouse second by putting away or leaving.

> *Every divorce begins with one spouse putting the other away. If they never put the other away, there would never be a divorce.*

Paul goes further and explains another reason why the believer should not put the unbeliever away *if the unbeliever is willing or pleased to live with the believer.* It's in v. 14, which has to do with the sanctification of the partner and the family. That's a very important reason to remain married.

However, Paul gives another reason why he words it that way. It's in v. 15.

[15] But if the unbelieving depart, let him depart. A brother or a sister is <u>not under bondage</u> in such cases: but God hath called us to peace.

Before I explain this verse, let me point out one thing: God doesn't like abandonment. If a spouse leaves and abandons -- let them go. As we will see next, you are free from them. You can go on in life and remarry. God doesn't look favorably on abandonment. Do you know why? It's the opposite of his character. His character is, "I will never leave you or forsake you" (Hebrews 13:5). God is not into abandonment.

Did you catch what Paul just said? If the unbelieving spouse doesn't want to stay in this marriage, then let them go. And then he uses an interesting phrase -- he says the believing spouse, "is *not under bondage* in such cases" (NIV says, "is not *bound* in such circumstances"). Bound, bondage -- to what? What is he talking about? He touches it later in this chapter in v. 39:

1 Corinthians 7:39 (KJV - underline added)
[39] The wife is <u>bound</u> by the law as long as her husband liveth; but if her husband be dead, she is at liberty to be married to whom she will; only in the Lord.

He also says the same thing in Romans 7:1-3:

Romans 7:1-3 (KJV - underline added)
[1] Know ye not, brethren, (for I speak to them that know the law,) how that the law hath dominion over a man as long as he liveth? [2] For the woman which hath an husband is <u>bound</u> by the law to her husband so long as he liveth; but if the husband be dead, she is <u>loosed</u> from the law of her husband. [3] So then if, while her husband liveth, she be married to another man, she shall be called an adulteress: but if her husband be

dead, she is free from that law; so that she is no adulteress, though she be married to another man.

In 1 Corinthians 7:39 and Romans 7:1-3, Paul is talking about the Old Testament Law, and the only way to be released from marriage according to the Law was through the death of one of the spouses or a writing of divorce (Deuteronomy 24). The death aspect is what is being addressed in both passages:

1 Corinthians 7:39 (KJV - underline added)
[39] The wife is <u>bound</u> by the law as long as her husband liveth.

Romans 7:2 (KJV - underline added)
[2] For the woman which hath an husband is <u>bound</u> by the law to her husband so long as he liveth; but if the husband be dead, she is <u>loosed</u> from the law of her husband.

> **If the unbelieving spouse doesn't want to stay in this marriage, then let them go. And then he uses an interesting phrase -- he says the believing spouse, "is not under bondage in such cases".**

The word that Paul uses in 1 Corinthians 7:15 that is translated "under bondage" is, "douloo". It is a derivative of the Greek word he used in 1 Corinthians 7:39, and Romans 7:2. That word is "deo", which is translated "bound". "Deo" and "Douloo" are in the same family of words, and both portray various aspects of the same thing. So Paul hasn't changed his position on anything; he's saying the same thing in all three scriptures. He's simply showing the different aspects of being "bound" versus being "under bondage". For example: the end result of being bound by chains verses being under the bondage of chains is the same -- the person is tied up with chains.

Paul is using the same verbiage in v. 15 when he says that if the unbeliever departs, the remaining spouse is not "under bondage" or "bound" in those situations. So, getting away from the technical approach of what words Paul is using, what is he saying? He's saying this:

Here is another situation where a spouse is to be released from the covenant of marriage. It is when an unbelieving spouse leaves. If that happens, let them go. We are allowed to live a life of peace in those situations. In light of the other two scriptures that deal with the word "bound" (1 Corinthians 7:39 and Romans 7:2), Paul is saying that if a person has an unbelieving husband or wife who leaves them because of the difference in beliefs, that believer is as free to remarry as they would be if their spouse had died (1 Corinthians 7:39, and Romans 7:2). They are "released" from being "bound" to a person in marriage and free to marry a different person.

In reality, if you look closely at all three of these scriptures, Paul really isn't saying anything new. It's the same thing Jesus said in the gospels. When an unbeliever leaves a marriage, they have typically already "put away" the believer before they ever left. They are leaving the believer because they have chosen someone or something else to be first in their life. They broke the covenant with the believer by not keeping them "first" in their life. To let them go in peace (which will ultimately end in divorce) makes sense, because the covenant has already been broken when the unbeliever put away the believer for whatever reason they were leaving.

I add this bit of insight because it can be overlooked: in 1 Corinthians 7:39, Paul is not talking about ex-husbands. He's talking about people who are still married -- husbands. If you take the earlier verses in chapter 7:12-16 -- and what was said about a situation where an unbelieving spouse leaves -- the believing spouse is free of the marriage the same way they'd be free of the marriage if the spouse had died. If we combine those verses with v. 39, it is saying that in either case: (1.) the husband died; or (2.) he left. In either situation the woman is not "bound", which makes her free to remarry. Here is the entire verse:

1 Corinthians 7:39 (NIV - underline added)
[39] A woman is bound to her husband as long as he lives. But <u>if her husband dies, she is free to marry anyone she wishes, but he must belong to the Lord.</u>

The only stipulation Paul put on the remarriage is this: when you remarry, don't make the same mistake you made the first time. Don't marry an unbeliever. The new spouse "<u>must belong to the Lord.</u>"

If she or he wasn't bound in 7:15 when the unbeliever left, and they are not "bound" in v. 39 if the spouse died -- and the word "bound" or "under bondage" are different facets of the same thing in both scriptures -- we know Paul is saying the same result is Ok in both situations. If a spouse abandons (v. 15) you (or puts you away for whatever reason), or should a spouse dies (v. 39), in either case you are not "bound". You are free to remarry.

Again, like it said earlier in chapter 7:12-16, I'm very confident the principle in v. 39 is not just for women. It's for men, also. The reason Paul said it that way was because a woman didn't have the right to put away and divorce a husband. She had to wait until he did something about the marriage. We know the man had the right to put her away and divorce her. He could end being "bound" in the marriage, but she couldn't. In v. 15 & 39, Paul specifically addresses women. Why? It was a huge change in their culture for a woman to be given the right to declare she is "not bound" to her husband, move on with her life, and get remarried if she desired. In the past, that had been reserved only for men. Now, Paul says, a woman can do it, too. That was earth-shattering for the women. So, Paul addressed it and talked about it -- talking directly to the women.

To my knowledge, that is the majority of scriptures in the Old and New Testament that deal directly with putting away and the divorce of a spouse. If I've missed one, I'm quite confident it doesn't say anything different than what we've already discovered from the passages we've looked at.

With that in mind, it's time to draw some conclusions on this subject. I will endeavor to do that in the next chapter.

Summary and Application

Chapter 8

Now I'm going to take what we've learned and review the major points as well as make a few more applications to show how these principles apply to our culture today. Bear with me; some of what I've already written, I will repeat here. This is such a huge concept, many of the main points may be missed if I don't remind you of them, so I'm repeating some things. The areas we're looking at here will hopefully help clarify some of the many, many questions surrounding this subject.

1.) The marriage relationship is based on the concept of "covenant".

The union of marriage, from God's perspective, is not based on a marriage license that was filed at the county courthouse or the government's recognition of two people being married. Marriage from God's perspective is all about covenant. He views it from the covenant perspective. He handles it as a covenant. God absolutely does not see it as a contract.

Most people in the Western world carry the mindset that marriage is like a contract. That's the core of the problem. It's one of the reasons why so many marriages struggle. Most people go into it totally unaware of and unprepared for the scope of change that will need to take place in them for the marriage to work. Even if the couple stays together, the amount of devastation that occurs from not knowing how to relate with each other often devastates the relationship.

I've counseled so many people who struggled with their marriage because their expectations were not being met. The relationship turned into something that was different than what they agreed to before they were married. This lack of having our expectations met is all based on a contract mentality. The other person was not holding up their end of the contract, and it was not sitting well with them. They had no concept of what a covenant was to look or function like.

2.) What is a covenant?

The heart and soul of a covenant is typically referred to as the "great exchange". Covenant is when one person or party gives up their personal rights to invest their life into another person or party. The other person absolutely becomes first in everything. Every decision, plan, goal, dream, purpose, and desire includes the other person. It also goes beyond that and puts them first in how all of life plays out. This is a mutual agreement between both people. Covenant is not built on what I should or can get from this relationship. It's built on what I am bringing and can give to the other person in this relationship. If that is not the mindset of both partners, the concept of covenant will not work. One will be taken advantage of while the other becomes the king or queen being served.

When the mindset of covenant is in place, conversations and decision-making happen totally differently. Everything is approached from the angle of, "How can I make the other person happy and meet their needs?" For example, if you are going out to eat, deciding where to eat will sound something like this:

> Husband: "Where would you like to eat?"
> Wife: "I chose last time. You choose this time."
> Husband: "What are you hungry for?"
> Wife: "It doesn't matter to me, I'll do whatever you would
> like."
> Husband: "No, just tell me what you would like, and we can go
> there."
> Wife: "No, I picked what we did last time. This time you
> decide."

It becomes almost an argument based on how I can serve you and make you happy. Most arguments in a marriage are based on what I want vs. what you want, so we begin arguing and trying to convince the other to do it our way. In covenant, the opposite takes place. We are intentionally trying to place ourselves second in an effort to place the other person first.

This approach should happen in every area of life: vacations, new purchases, plans for the day together, long term goals, how the money is spent, etc.

As you can easily see, if both partners are not approaching the marriage equally in the desire to serve the other, someone will be taken advantage of. Covenant is not one person serving the other most of the time, and occasionally they are thrown a scrap. Covenant is an equal exchange of two people approaching every situation and decision from the perspective of, "I want to serve my spouse and make this about them."

Covenant can be summarized as a person giving up their life for another. It is placing them first in priority and meeting their needs before

221

any other person or thing. The mindset of covenant is to invest oneself into the other person and do everything in our power to fulfill them: spirit, soul, and body. I realize as humans, we are limited as to what we can do to meet the needs of our partner -- spiritually. God is ultimately the one who fulfills every individual human being, and to look to a person to accomplish that is very unhealthy. However, we do have an affect on each other's spiritual lives. Even the simple concept of whether we are willing to pray together and come into agreement with each other will have a spiritual affect on our partner. Don't discount the spiritual affect we have on each other.

Covenant is a way of thinking that is opposite of how we typically view marriage in our Western culture. These are the type of questions that are a normal part of problem solving in a covenant marriage:

> *Covenant can be summarized as a person giving up their life for another. It is placing them first in priority and meeting their needs before any other person or thing.*

> "What do you need from me?"

"How can I help make that happen for you?"

"What do I need to do?"

"Are you OK now?"

Our focus is not what I need from them; it's how can I be of help to them?

I can't restate this point often enough: the giving has to be done equally -- between both partners. It cannot become one person serving the other. When it's done correctly, those questions will cause a multitude of good things to take place in the marriage. The spouse will feel valued and loved. They will realize their viewpoint and opinion is important and the other person wants to hear what they have to say. They will be given the freedom to express themselves without interruption or contradiction. Any anger that comes from feeling unimportant or not being heard will go away. They will realize they are safe, and the other person is not trying to take advantage of them.

Covenants are designed and intended to be a life-long agreement. They are not to be broken until the death of one of the testators (partners in the covenant). However, because we live in a world where not everything plays out as intended or planned, God in his love, mercy, and graciousness has made provision for the situations where one person is too selfish or immature to make the choice to live this marriage out in a covenant fashion. That way the violence and abuse can stop, and both partners can move on in their lives forgiven and with hope for the future.

3.) What breaks a covenant?

When does the "great exchange" cease to exist? It ends when the exchange process of putting each other at the highest level of priority stops; when one or both parties place someone or something else as the first priority in their life. The person with whom they made covenant is no longer the prime focus of life. They are now demoted in importance to the 2nd, 3rd, 5th, or even 10th place of importance, and other things or people come before them. That is what scripture calls putting or sending away. Someone has been put or sent away from their position of being first, and someone or something else has taken their place.

Let me add, this is not an off the cuff, had a bad day, lost my senses for a while type of thing we're talking about. This is an attitude that has developed over a period of time, and it is set in concrete. In other words, one person has made up their mind, and they're not going to change it. They don't want help. They don't want the original agreement, and they are making decisions and living in a way that puts the other in a much lower position of importance in their life. As far as they're concerned, it's going to stay that way.

We see an example of this is Jeremiah 3 where God divorced Israel. When we looked at this scripture before, but we didn't look at the surrounding verses. Here's what they say.

Jeremiah 3:1-15 (AMP - underline added)
[1] THAT IS to say, If a man puts away his wife and she goes from him and becomes another man's, will he return to her again? [Of course not!] Would not that land [where such a thing happened] be greatly polluted? But you have played the harlot [against Me] with many lovers — yet would you now return to Me? says the Lord [or do you even think to return to Me?]
[2] Lift up your eyes to the bare heights and see. Where have you not been adulterously lain with? By the wayside you have sat waiting for lovers [eager for idolatry], like an Arabian [desert tribesman who waits to plunder] in the wilderness; and you have polluted the land with your vile harlotry and your wickedness (unfaithfulness and disobedience to God).
[3] Therefore the showers have been withheld, and there has been no spring rain. Yet you have the brow of a prostitute; you refuse to be ashamed.
[4] Have you not just now cried to Me: My Father, You were the guide and companion of my youth?
[5] Will He retain His anger forever? Will He keep it to the end? Behold, you have so spoken, but you have done all the evil things you could and have had your way and have carried them through.

[6] *Moreover, the Lord said to me [Jeremiah] in the days of Josiah the king [of Judah], Have you seen what that faithless and backsliding Israel has done — how she went up on every high hill and under every green tree and there played the harlot?*

[7] *And I said, After she has done all these things, she will return to Me; but she did not return, and her faithless and treacherous sister Judah saw it.*

[8] *And I saw, even though [Judah knew] that for this very cause of committing adultery (idolatry) I [the Lord] had put faithless Israel away and given her a bill of divorce; yet her faithless and treacherous sister Judah was not afraid, but she also went and played the harlot [following after idols].*

[9] *And through the infamy and unseemly frivolity of Israel's whoredom [because her immorality mattered little to her], she polluted and defiled the land, [by her idolatry] committing adultery with [idols of] stones and trees.*

[10] *But in spite of all this, her faithless and treacherous sister Judah did not return to Me in sincerity and with her whole heart, but only in sheer hypocrisy [has she feigned obedience to King Josiah's reforms], says the Lord. [2Ch 34:33; Ho 7:13,14.]*

[11] *And the Lord said to me, Backsliding and faithless Israel has shown herself less guilty than false and treacherous Judah.*

[12] *Go and proclaim these words toward the north [where the ten tribes have been taken as captives] and say, Return, faithless Israel, says the Lord, and I will not cause My countenance to fall and look in anger upon you, for I am merciful, says the Lord; I will not keep My anger forever.*

[13] *Only know, understand, and acknowledge your iniquity and guilt — that you have rebelled and transgressed against the Lord your God and have scattered your favors among strangers under every green tree, and you have not obeyed My voice, says the Lord.*

[14] *Return, O faithless children [of the whole twelve tribes], says the Lord, for I am Lord and Master and Husband to you, and I will take*

you [not as a nation, but individually] — one from a city and two from a tribal family — and I will bring you to Zion. [Lk 15:20-22.]
[15] And I will give you [spiritual] shepherds after My own heart [in the final time], who will feed you with knowledge and understanding and judgment.

We're not talking about a quick, off the cuff decision or change in relationship (seen all through this passage). Contrary to what society may think, covenant is not created when we say "I do," and it's not broken when we say "I won't." This is like everything else in scripture: a heart attitude that has formed over time.

Here is a simple verse-by-verse explanation to bring the thought of this section of scripture into our time.

v. 1 - This is referring back to the law and what was said in Deuteronomy 24:1-4 (specifically v. 4). In that culture, once the putting away and divorce had taken place, if the same two people wanted to remarry again at a later time, they were forbidden to do so.

God is referencing that and applying it to the situation with Israel. Even though they were not divorced yet, Israel had definitely broken covenant and put God away at this point. God is asking if they will come back to Him, or even have a desire to come back to Him.

v. 2 - God calls their "unfaithfulness and disobedience" to Him the same as adultery. Now we have a clear understanding of what caused the covenant between Israel and God to be broken. The people were not faithful to God in their service to Him, and they chose instead to do what they wanted and became disobedient.

This is wicked and adulterous to God. He was telling them that they were living in these things everywhere they went, and from His perspective they really didn't care what He thought.

v. 3 - As God, He said He was withholding some of the rain for their crops because of what they were doing. God is saying He wasn't fully investing Himself into their lives now that they had put Him away. He hoped to get their attention and that they would change their minds and behavior, but they were unaffected by it and stubbornly went on doing their own thing without any shame.

v. 4 - They obviously felt the results of not getting enough rain for their crops, so they went back to God and tried to make a case or manipulate Him by saying, "You've been our guide, and we've been companions since our youth."

v. 5 - They continue by saying, "Are you going to stay angry forever? Aren't you ever going to let go of your anger, or are you just going to hold on to it?" They twisted the situation and in es - sence said the relationship problem was God's fault -- He needs to stop being so angry. However, they hadn't owned their behavior, nor repented of it.

Sounds kind of like a typical marriage fight: blame shifting, no ownership of wrong, no hint of changing the things that are being done that are destroying the relationship.

v. 6 - God talked to Jeremiah (the prophet) about it.

v. 7 - God tells Jeremiah that He wanted the best and was trying to be patient. God hoped that after Israel had been disobedient for a while, she would come back and restore the relationship,

> *Contrary to what society may think, covenant is not created when we say "I do," and it's not broken when we say "I won't." This is like everything else in scripture: a heart attitude that has formed over time.*

but she had not. To make matters worse, her sister -- who also was being faithless and treacherous to God -- had now seen what was happening.

There are two things we need to see here: first, God was not having a bad day or just making some kind of hasty decision when Israel made one mistake. God gave a lot of time to this relationship hoping she would change her behavior. This is the example we need to follow. Covenants are not broken with a single action, mistake, or bad choice. In fact, these things can go on for a period of time and the covenant still remain intact.

Secondly, the thing that breaks a marriage covenant today is the same thing God was looking for -- an attitude or heart change by one or both of the spouses. Like I said above, this is an attitude that has developed over a period of time, and it is set in concrete. In other words, one person (or both) has made up their mind, and they're not going to change it. They don't want help. They don't want to change the devastating and violating thinking, choices, and behaviors. They've decided to live their life however they want to, and it doesn't make any difference what the other person thinks. Serving the other person is no longer first to them. They are serving themselves first -- they've been doing it for a while -- and from all indications, it's not going to change. That's what breaks a covenant.

v. 8 -   Why was God concerned about Judah? I don't want to go into this deeply, but I'll briefly address it. Originally, the 12 tribes were one nation called Israel. Problems developed in the nation, and there was a split. Ten tribes in the north stayed in unity and formed the northern kingdom, and two tribes in the south split away and formed the southern kingdom. The north remained known as Israel, and the south was called Judah. Technically, all twelve tribes were still the offspring of Jacob or Israel. They were all still God's people. In covenant, God had committed Himself to all of them (not just the northern ten tribes).

So, God was married to Judah (the southern two tribes) as well as Israel (the ten northern tribes). However, since the kingdom had split, God was dealing with them separately. If you study the concept of God being married to all twelve tribes of Israel, then divorcing the northern ten tribes but seemingly not Judah -- even though she had broken the covenant, too -- you can see how God desired to bring Judah back into covenant relationship with Him and also remarry the northern ten tribes (also called Israel). You will find this discussed in numerous places in the Old Testament (Hosea, Jeremiah, Ezekiel, and Isaiah 40-55).

That's why God was concerned about the example that Israel (the northern ten tribes) was setting for Judah (the southern two tribes). He didn't want to lose all twelve tribes, or as He referred to them, both "sisters". He didn't want to lose both of them to divorce.

Some feel the reason God didn't divorce Judah -- even though her actions were worse than her sister Israel's -- is because He would have lost the spouse through whom the Savior would ultimately be born. Jesus came from the tribe of Judah. Judah had clearly put God away by her choices and actions, but He refused to step away from the "marriage" for the sake of bringing the future Savior into the world.

This point always brings up a question: should I stay legally married -- even though I'm put away -- for the greater good (and there are many different scenarios of what the "greater good" might be)? I can't answer that question. That is ultimately going to be a decision between you and God. However, there is a precedent for staying in the marriage legally, even though the covenant has been broken. God gave the example right here. With Judah, He stayed in the marriage; with Israel, He divorced her.

However, it is clear in this scripture that it was because Israel (the ten tribes) had broken faith or covenant with God that He put her away and divorced her.

v. 9 - Israel was very open and flagrant about how she was treating God.

v. 10 - Though Judah watched Israel do wrong, she didn't sincerely return to God either -- just hypocritically or in pretense.

v. 11 - God says Judah was guiltier than Israel.

v. 12 - God pleads for Israel to return to Him again (remarry).

v. 13 - Through their disobedience the covenant was broken. Through acknowledging the wrong and repentance, the marriage could be restored.

This is another example for us today. If a marriage gets into trouble, the only way it can be truly restored is if the parties acknowledge the wrong, repent or turn away from the wrong things that were done, and begin doing what is right -- not in pretense or hypocrisy, but from the heart.

I've seen so many couples try to restore their marriage when one of them is just playing a game. They don't REALLY want to fix it, but they do want to avoid the divorce courts, not lose their property and finances, remain looking good in the community or the church, keep the wife as the mommy for the home and children -- but also have their mistress

I went through all of that explanation so that we'd see one main point: God was not hasty in His decision to "put away" and "divorce" Israel. He wasn't just struggling emotionally for a day or two. This was a long and drawn-out decision.

(and on and on the reasons can go). As we all know, this approach doesn't work. Hypocrisy and pretense didn't work with God, and it shouldn't work with us either.

v. 14 - God pleads with both of them to return to Him.

v. 15 - Here, God gives one of the reasons for shepherds or pastors. God wants a faithful and obedient people. Pastors play a role in keeping believers on track with God and out of sin in their own lives.

I went through all of that explanation so that we'd see one main point: God was not hasty in His decision to put away and divorce Israel. He wasn't just struggling emotionally for a day or two. This was a long and drawn-out decision that God made, and it was a decision that He would have gladly stopped, had Israel sincerely returned to Him. The point is, if we go through this kind of decision, it can't be made hastily or quickly, leaving no room for restoration. God gives the example of the correct approach.

231

#4 - God is not against divorce; He's against putting away.

Before you read this point, please slow down and understand what I'm about to say. Neither putting away nor divorce was ever supposed to happen. It was never part of God's design. No one was ever to end up in divorce court. God's intention for a marriage was that the two would never be "put asunder" in any way, by any one (Matthew 19:6). *Technically, God isn't in favor of putting away or divorce"*. But because the understanding of this subject has become so messed up, I stated it the way I did in the point above: God is not against divorce; He's against putting away.

Even though neither one was supposed to ever happen, they did. Now God has to deal with something that is less than His perfect design. In scripture, God places the emphasis of what displeases Him on *putting away*. It is not on divorce. Why? Does He like one more than the other? No. As we've said over and over, the core of the problem is in the heart of the person who puts the other away. The paper work (divorce) is the after effect. As the scripture shows, because of people's hard hearts, there are times God actually wants the paper work (divorce) to happen to protect the victim. But let's be honest -- if He had His way, neither putting away nor divorce would take place.

Now that we've studied both words in Scripture and seen how God views both of them, the surprising conclusion is that God *never said divorce* was the issue. He *did say* that *putting away* is the real issue. That may not be news to some, but there may others who have never thought of it that way. Let's look at it a little more.

The main word we hear in America is "divorce". We don't hear much of anything about putting away. As a result, we think the whole thing falls under the word divorce and that God is against it. End of subject. Scripturally, that is not true. God is always against the putting away process, but there are situations where God is actually in agreement that a couple needs to divorce. As a general rule, God agrees that a written "bill of divorcement" (in our society, that's the same as going to court and getting a legal divorce) should be given if one partner has been put away and the initiator refuses help or reconciliation in the marriage. According to Malachi 2:14-16, God sees this as the victim having violence done against them. They are covered and wrapped in on-going violation or violence as they would be covered with a garment. That's what God hates.

> *Neither putting away nor divorce was ever supposed to happen.*
>
> *It was never part of God's design.*

"Putting Away" and "Divorce" are two separate steps in the same process. They are the steps that transpire when a marriage covenant is broken. Putting away or breaking the covenant makes God very angry, while the written certificate of divorce doesn't seem to bother God much at all. In fact, He seems to encourage it if someone has been put away or is being violated. We saw it emphasized in the Old Testament, and Jesus also emphasized it in the New Testament -- if you are going to put someone away and force them to live in that state of personal, covenant violation, then give them a written divorce. Don't just put them away. Set them free from the abuse and violation that comes from having been put away so they can move on in life.

From God's perspective, getting the divorce at the courthouse is not the sin. The sin happened long before that paperwork was ever filed. It happened when one or both put the other away. That's the part that God hates; not the written papers that says it's over.

I personally believe that God is thoroughly disgusted with many, if not most, of our so-called "marriages". Just because society, the church, the legal system, and the IRS consider a couple to be married, doesn't mean they are still in covenant in God's eyes. Allow me give a few examples that I've seen.

I said this before, but it's worth repeating: when a couple lives individual lives in their "marriage", it's clear there is no covenant left between them. They do most everything separately: friendships, finances, household work and chores, entertainment, leisure activities, vacations, transportation, and on and on the list can go. I knew one couple who came to church for almost every service -- but they rarely rode in the same vehicle. They drove separately. Why? They didn't like to be together that much. They had separate bank accounts. They also had separate goals in life. To me they had obviously put each other away, and you guessed it; it was only a matter of time before they divorced.

What about sleeping arrangements? Or to be more direct, what about the couples sexual life? Sexual intimacy in a marriage should never stop. Even if one partner is no longer physically capable for some reason, in an effort to express love and continue to serve the other person and meet their needs, some form of sexual intimacy should be taking place. Sleeping arrangements often reflect sexual intimacy. I realize in some cases there are legitimate, medical reasons to sleep in separate beds or bedrooms. However, from my experience, in medical situations the sex life still remains active and alive even if they aren't physically sleeping in the same bed. I'm not talking about those situations. I'm talking about the couple that hasn't had sex in months or even years because they have no desire for each other, nor do they have a desire to serve each other in the sexual way. Scripturally, someone (or both) in that marriage has put the other away. Once it has gone on for months and the attitude is set that the sexual aspect of the relationship is over, I believe the covenant is broken and probably has been for quite some time.

The Apostle Paul says this:

1Corinthians 7:1-5 (NIV)
[1] Now for the matters you wrote about: It is good for a man not to marry. [2] But since there is so much immorality, each man should have his own wife, and each woman her own husband. [3] The husband should fulfill his marital duty to his wife, and likewise the wife to her husband. [4] The wife's body does not belong to her alone but also to her husband. In the same way, the husband's body does not belong to him alone but also to his wife. [5] Do not deprive each other except by mutual consent and for a time, so that you may devote yourselves to prayer (KJV - "fasting and prayer"). Then come together again so that Satan will not tempt you because of your lack of self-control.

Paul is talking about the sexual aspect of the marriage relationship. In marriage, Paul says there needs to be a healthy sex life. In a covenant, neither spouse has the right to tell the other one, "No," when it comes to an active sex life. Once in covenant, your body is not your own (v.3-4). He also says that the husband needs to "fulfill his marital duty", and so does the wife (v. 3). This is talking about having sex. He actually calls it a "marital duty." Wow. That sounds cold. Why would he say it that way? He's talking covenant language here. Remember, in covenant, our focus becomes serving the other person and fulfilling them and their needs, desires, dreams, and goals. He's basically saying, "You married them, you're in covenant with them, so now fulfill that covenant by ministering to them sexually." Then in verse 4-5, he says you have no right to deprive the other person of sex.

He gives only one exception to this. The sex life can be stopped "by mutual consent" if one person wants to devote themselves to God in "fasting and prayer". The KJV has the correct translation here. The NIV only uses the word "prayer". That is not correct. In the original

235

Greek it says both fasting and prayer. And please notice: this isn't one person's decision to stop the sexual intimacy. It is "by mutual consent" (KJV -- "with consent"). Both people need to agree to this. To me, God is giving a time limit here as to how long a couple can go without having sex. It's tied to how long you are able to or have fasted (gone without food for the purpose of devotion to God in prayer). Some people have fasted up to 40 days. So in their case, if the spouse agrees, they could abstain from sex for up to 40 days. Other people have never fasted more than a few days at a time, or at all. That again is the time indicator as to how long you as a couple can abstain from sex (to pursue God -- not simply just stop having sex) if you both agree on it. You decide for yourself. But one thing is absolutely clear: the idea of being married but not having sex for months and years at a time is not scriptural. It is a breach of covenant. Part of the covenant that God announced was they would be "one flesh" (Genesis 2:24; Matthew 19:5). That's talking about the sexual part. Once that aspect of the covenant is abandoned or withheld by one or both of the partners, you have broken the covenant. One (or both) has put the other away -- sexually.

5.) Is divorce a sin?

Sadly, what we usually hear in Christianity is that getting a divorce is a sin; and not just a sin -- it's a sin of the worst kind.

Let me make a big statement again: divorce can't be a sin, because God is divorced. GOD CANNOT SIN. God divorced Israel. He is a divorcee. Remember, in Jeremiah 3:6-9, God put away the nation of Israel and gave her a bill of divorcement.

I realize that Israel precipitated this, but the bottom line is that God initiated the ending of the marriage by divorcing Israel and putting her away. The blanket statement that says divorce is sin can't be right -- because then God would be a sinner.

There is something else of interest that we should note here. In the New Testament, Jesus said if unfaithfulness was involved, the innocent spouse could put away the other without giving them a written divorce. But notice what God did: even though unfaithfulness had been involved with Israel, he put her away and also gave her a bill of divorce. Why? I'm not sure, it doesn't say. But it is a good example to follow in our culture. Even if there has been unfaithfulness, don't just put the other away -- give them the legal divorce.

I've seen situations where the innocent spouse refused to agree to a divorce after the other had been unfaithful, but neither did they want to be involved with the sexual aspect of the marriage anymore. The spouse who had not committed adultery wanted to punish the guilty party for what they had done. In essence they put the unfaithful partner away, and treated them horribly in many ways -- not just in the sexual aspect, but by refusing to agree to a divorce. It was their way of punishing their spouse and getting revenge. Here's God's opinion on that: GET A DIVORCE and end it. Move on in life rather than living in a continual state of bitterness, unforgiveness, and revenge.

Another reason it can't always be a sin is that God would not have recommended it in the Law (Deuteronomy 24:1-2). He can't tell someone to sin and remain righteous. Jesus agreed with this in the New Testament (Matthew 19:3-9; Mark 10:2-12 -- please reference chapter 7).

Some religions, through their traditions, make some sins to be worse than others, even though this cannot be found in scripture. Sin is sin. There is no place where one sin is talked about as if it's no big deal, or acceptable, but another one is a big deal and absolutely unacceptable. Any and all sin causes us to fall short of the glory of God.

Yet in Christianity -- whether we are Protestant, Catholic, Anglican, or otherwise -- some sins are deemed to be far worse than others. Divorce seems to always fall into the list of sins that are absolutely the worst. Since this ranking of sin isn't in the Bible, we must conclude that God doesn't think or feel that way. He doesn't see some sins as "more sinful" or "more worthy of judgment" than others. Now, Scripture does show that some sins have more consequences in life and society than others. For example, getting caught stealing a candy bar from Walmart will not have as severe of consequences as getting a DUI or DWI. Then again, getting a DUI or DWI doesn't carry the consequences of being proven guilty of murder. Yet in God's eyes, the Bible simply says that stealing, drunkenness, and murder are all sin. It doesn't make one out to be worse than another.

Because of this foundational belief system that flows through the Christian church (Protestant, Catholic, or Anglican), divorce carries a huge stigma among most believers. I'm not saying that divorce should be glorified, but I will make a scriptural statement that may shock you a bit.

Divorce should not *always* be viewed as a *bad thing*, and there are times it should be viewed as a *good thing*.

Now that you've picked yourself up off the floor, let me explain. When God divorced Israel, no one could say that God did a bad thing. In fact, it had to be a good thing, because God did it, right? The very reason God allowed divorce to happen in the Old Testament -- which was to protect and release the victim from further violation and abuse, which Jesus also agreed with in the New Testament when He confirmed and upheld the laws regarding marriage -- is a good thing. The *reason* God had to do it was bad: it was because of the hardness of people's hearts. To this day, that is likely the biggest reason people divorce -- hardness of heart. That hardness of heart became the reason God decided to do something that He really didn't want to do. The decision God made to allow people to divorce -- knowing their hearts were hard and that forcing them to stay together would only cause prolonged victimization and violence -- was a good decision.

There have been numerous times over the years of ministry where I've seen a divorce as a good thing. The most obvious usually involves some type of abuse (especially if it's sexual abuse) -- whether of the children or the spouse. From my experience, when it comes to children, it's usually the man who is the perpetrator, but that is not a general rule. Mothers can also abuse their children. Stop and think about this: consider a family where one of the parents is physically, psychologically, and emotionally abusing one or more of the children through sexual abuse (both boys and girls). The covenant is obviously already broken with the spouse. Is it actually better for the victim to remain in that situation and keep their children in a place where they are being violated in spirit, soul, and body on an on-going basis, just so they can say they are still married? So they can say they haven't divorced? Really?

My advice has always been, at the very least, get a divorce, and if you have the proof, put the perpetrator behind bars. Why get the legal system involved? Because if that person is willing to do it to their own children, they will perpetrate again in a

> *Divorce should not __always__ be viewed as a __bad thing__, and there are times it should be viewed as a __good thing__.*

different setting. Yes, I agree they need help, but they also need to be stopped. I've watched men come out of previous marriages where they had been sexually involved with the children. They didn't go to jail, but it ended in a divorce. These same men would remarry and begin to do the same thing with the new children in the family.

In those situations, if the man (or woman) is unwilling to get help and change, divorce is not just the only option; it is also a good thing.

Now let's look at the other side.To say divorce is NEVER wrong would be an over-statement. There are times it is a wrong part of the process. Look at it this way: anytime something flows from a hard heart, it can't be righteous or of God, which means it's wrong. But let's be real, much of what the human race does exudes from a hard heart. Let's not label one thing as *so* ungodly, but yet hang on to other areas of our lives that come from the same hard heart. I'm not saying this as an excuse to be involved in sin, but it is a reality check to help keep a correct perspective. To say divorce is wrong yet permit lying, cheating, stealing, abuse, or deceit -- which come from the same hard heart -- is to be hypocritical. Whatever the hard heart of a person puts out, it's all equally bad.

Just as a reminder: in the Greek, the fornication to which God is opposed is not just sexual activity; it also includes the concept of idolatry (Jesus referred to fornication in Matt. 5:32, 19:9). The things that God referenced in Jeremiah 2-3 -- and His attitude and response to them through the divorce -- makes the idolatry point very understandable. God likened their idolatry to adultery, which is part of the overall concept of fornication, to which Jesus referred in the above references. Having too strong a love, desire, or admiration for a thing or person -- to the extent that the thing becomes more important than agreement with the spouse -- can also be considered fornication.

I've seen this play out in so many ways.

Let me give you some examples.

I watched a Christian woman have such a strong desire for fashion that she changed her wardrobe excessively, despite her husband's pleading for her to stop. She jeopardized the family financially by getting them deeper and deeper into debt, depriving the family of other things in order to dress herself (and sometimes the children) in the latest, most popular fashions. In reality, she was committing fornication with those clothes and fashion. They had become an idol to her. She had put her husband away for them. They were more important to her, and she had made them a higher priority than what her husband desired or what the family needed financially.

That's a form of putting the spouse away in fornication that has nothing to do with having sex with someone else. With her it revolved around clothes. It can happen with anything from re-decorating the house, to being a wife who is shopping every chance she gets, to living vicariously through her children, to being overly active in the church or community, and on the list can go. Once we overrule or ignore the Godly pleading and desires of our spouse to do what we want or consider it more important no matter what the spouse may say -- we are playing around with what the Bible calls "fornication".

> *To say divorce is NEVER wrong would be an over-statement.*

Here's an example that has to do with guys.

I've watched this happen in numerous settings and with a number of guys. Hunting or fishing becomes more important than their spouse and family. When that time of the year comes, it's like they're obsessed.

241

Everything stops so they can hunt or fish.It doesn't matter what the wife or family may need, he's is going to do his thing and everybody will need to accept that whether they like it or not. He gets extremely stubborn about it. Fights break out over it. Church and God absolutely take second place to it. Looking in from the outside, it's obvious that life has definitely become ALL ABOUT HIM for this period of time. He may not be having sex with another woman, but God views that as fornication in that marriage. It will produce bad things. Again, just like with the woman's example above, it can happen with anything or any type of activity. It's not the thing or activity that is the problem, it's what is in the heart of the man.

The examples show the fact that both people are really struggling with selfishness. Now that you understand what covenant is about, it's easy to see that selfishness and covenant do not work together. They are op-posites. The same attitudes can prevail whether they're in the husband or the wife. This is not a gender specific thing. It doesn't make a lot difference to them if it damages their relationship with their spouse or the family. They will say it does, but their actions and choices prove otherwise. It doesn't matter that they have little time or finances left over to invest into other areas of the marriage. It doesn't matter that they are spending more than their share of the money on something they may or may not be able to afford. What matters to them is that they are doing what they want to do, and the spouse is going to need to either get used to it, or join them; but they're not going to change any-thing.

That attitude will eventually put the spouse away for the sports, hob-bies, cars, hunting, shopping, entertainment, etc. The spouse will come second, third, or less in value, priority, and importance compared to these other things. Once that sets in as a hard and fast attitude, it won't change. Their mind is made up. Now we're in the arena of breaking that marriage covenant through a form of fornication. Even though they haven't had sex with anyone but their spouse -- it's still considered fornication.

I want you to see that it's not just other people or physical affairs that can get in and break a covenant. A person can make "things" more important than their covenant partner, also. Once that begins happening in a marriage, the cavalry needs to ride in and save the marriage. If it isn't dealt with at that level, bigger problems are sure to develop, and one of the spouses will eventually put away and violate the other. Even if the abused spouse chooses to live with it, God is against it. Ultimately, if left unchecked, it will likely end in a divorce. The things that we may see as trivial disagreements in a marriage are nothing to play with. They are the things that grow and destroy what the relationship is supposed to be.

6.) Why has there been so much confusion over the subject?

The confusion seems to have come through the poor translations of the original Greek and Hebrew words. Interestingly, The King James Version does a lot better job than some of the newer versions. Yet in one passage that deals with the subject, the KJV also mistranslated putting away as divorce (Matt. 5:32). Most of the newer versions simply translate both Greek words "apoluo" and "apostasion" as divorce, as well as the Hebrew words "kereethooth" and "shalach" as divorce. It happened in both the Old and New Testaments.

Jesus remained consistent in what He said in the Gospels. He did not contradict the Law by stating that divorce ("apostasion") was sin. He said that putting away ("apoluo") was wrong.

Because of the incorrect translations, there has been a lot of confusion and misunderstanding. As we've already studied, they are two totally

243

separate words with totally different meanings in the Hebrew and Greek.

As a result, for the average Christian, divorce is viewed as the same thing as putting away. They are not the same. Putting away plays the biggest role in the process, since it actually starts the breakdown of the marriage. It then moves into the separation of the married partners in various forms, which is against the "becoming one" that God wanted to happen in a marriage.

> *It's not just other people or physical affairs that can get in and break a covenant. A person can also make "things" more important than their covenant partner.*

The writing or bill of divorce (the thing most people believe is the act of divorce) is actually the conclusion to the whole process. It's the part where the couple goes to court and legally finalizes the fact that their marriage is dead.

If these words are distinguished and the actual meaning of them is applied to the passages in scripture, the point the Bible is trying to get across to us becomes very clear.

For sake of clarification I will re-state something that may seem like a big statement for some of us. I need to keep re-stating this so it becomes very clear in our thinking. Do you realize that getting a divorce is never a sin from God's perspective? There is not one place in scripture where God says that He hates divorce or that it is a sin. What He *does* say is that He hates the sin of "putting away".

If we don't make that differentiation, we will never be able to clear up the confusion and misunderstandings that surround the issue.

7.) If a person is put away, God actually says a bill of divorce should be given.

The divorce paperwork that one files at the courthouse (bill of divorcement) is actually a step of freedom to the one who was put away. God actually sees this as a positive and necessary ending to a situation where someone has been put away. They can now move on and continue their life without being bound to a marriage in which the covenant has been broken. Since the two may be living together under the same roof, have a joint checking account, file joint on their income taxes, or have both names on the property, society still sees it as a marriage. But from God's perspective, if one has been put away, then the covenant is broken. If that doesn't get fixed, that union (marriage) no longer exists.

To force someone to stay in a relationship like that is not what God calls a marriage. Remember: marriage, from God's perspective, is actually a covenant. Once the covenant is broken, there is no marriage. Why would a loving God force the victim to stay in that relationship? He doesn't. If the marriage union is broken, God says we are to set the other free by giving them a divorce.

Both the Old and New Testaments agree on this. Jesus took the same stance. He never contradicted the Law by stating that "divorce" ("apostasion") was sin. He said that "putting away" ("apoluo") was sin. The Apostle Paul took the same stance in his writings.

In Matthew 19 and Mark 10, Jesus didn't dwell on the "divorce" aspect of a broken covenant. He dwelt on the putting away aspect -- because that is the core of the whole problem. The hardness of heart caused the

245

bad relationship, which resulted in abuse and violation. If a marriage is going to be fixed, it should not be done in the divorce stage; it should happen while the putting away, break, or separation is taking place. Once it's broken, why dwell on the divorce? The real problem occurred back in the time when it was falling apart. That is the putting away period of time.

Don't misunderstand my previous statement.Restoration can come even in the divorce stage, but it's going to be much more difficult to achieve once a couple is in the process of getting a legal divorce, or already are divorced. It would have been better to deal with the issue earlier. I bring that up because we tend to ignore all the red flags that indicate marriage problems. Too often, we act like they're not there and hope the problems go away. Then once the couple is actually considering filing papers, now we get all excited and try to stop it from happening. My point is that the signs of a problem were there all along. We should have gotten involved sooner.

8.) The core reason for broken covenants is hard hearts.

Jesus made it clear that "hardness of heart" was the reason for the commandment concerning putting away a spouse. And since putting away was the reason for the bill of divorcement, in essence, hardness of heart leads to both.

What does "hardness of heart" mean? In scripture, when God refers to a person as having a hard heart, He's saying they have become desensitized to what He wants -- His spiritual values and principles. In the deepest part of the person, they have become indifferent, callous, or hard to God's way of doing things.

When Jesus said the reason God allowed a person to put another away for "any and every reason" was because their hearts were hard, He was saying they didn't value God's priorities anyway. True covenant no longer existed in the relationship, so let them end it. He was not saying that God was in any way in favor of the union breaking up. He was saying that God saw "it is what it is," and someone was being violated or victimized. He decided it was better to let the two people go their separate ways for the sake of the victim.

Jesus made it clear that hardness of heart was the reason for the commandment concerning the bill of divorce. This is what was happening: men married women and later found themselves hating them. (Deuteronomy 22:13ff) Since they believed they couldn't get a divorce and still be right with God, (because of Genesis 2:23-25) they simply put the woman away. That way, they weren't divorced. They had the best of both worlds: the woman was out, and they were still all right with God.

The core reason for broken covenants is hard hearts.

This was absolute abuse. They were violating her as a human being by taking away the purpose for which she was created: to be a companion and helpmate. She was now sentenced to a life of ridicule, abandonment, loneliness, and in some cases, slavery. Since she was still legally married, if she went to another man (even if it was to merely help her family and herself physically survive) she was in adultery, because she didn't have a certificate or bill of divorcement. That was wrong. She needed to be able to move on in life but was being held prisoner to the bad marriage.

There is something very important for us to see, here. God *does* care about the person who is being mistreated and taken advantage of. He is not a hard and cruel taskmaster who is more concerned about His rules than the person. Religious thinking has turned that around. Similarly in Jesus' day, religion had turned the concept of the sabbath upside down by saying that people were here to serve the rules of the sabbath. Jesus said that was wrong; the sabbath was here to serve the people. The application is that people are not here to serve some standards or rules of marriage. Marriage is here to serve the people. *When that is no longer happening, God loves the people more than He loves the institution of marriage and all it's rules, and He releases the person from the institution.*

So for those of you who have felt like God abandoned you or betrayed you because your marriage fell apart, realize that is a man-made notion. People may have abandoned and condemned you, but God doesn't do that. God is more concerned about you than He is about holding you to a standard He set up. He already knew that human beings could not measure up to all the standards of righteousness. That's why He said this:

1John 1:9 (NIV)
[9] If we confess our sins, he is faithful and just and will forgive us our sins and purify us from all unrighteousness.

The human being messes up in every area of life -- including marriage. Just like in every other area, once something is so broken that it can no longer be fixed, God forgives. Why? So we can start over again. So we can go after it and give it another try. That's what forgiveness is all about. That principle applies to every area of our Christian life -- including marriage.

9 .) It may sound like I think divorce is a good thing.

It was never God's intention that the human race would have to deal with putting away or divorce. Neither one was in God's design and plan before sin entered the human race. So, in the sense of the original design and creation of marriage, neither putting away nor divorce is a good thing.

However, sin entered the picture and now we are dealing with a lot of things that God never intended, nor considers good. That's why Jesus came to shed His blood, so we could receive God's grace and forgiveness in a world and system that are very much not what God intended. I don't think either putting away or divorce is the best that God had intended, but because the world is what it is, divorce can be the lessor of the two evils from which we have to choose.

It was never God's design for the covenant to be broken and marriages to end in divorce. However, in some cases, I do think it's better than staying in a abusive, violating, victimizing relationship. I feel that way because God thinks in some cases it's better than staying in the relationship. Here are the examples we looked at:

> (1) Uncleanness/Fornication
>   - Deuteronomy 24:1-2; Matthew 19:9.
> (2) Violence/Abuse
>   - Deuteronomy 22:13-21; 24:1-2; Malachi 2:14-16
> (3) The Unbelieving Partner Leaving
>   - I Corinthians 7:12-16
> (4) Hardness of Heart (Often results in violation and abuse)
>   - Deuteronomy 22:13; 24:1-2; Matthew 5:31-32 & 19:3-9 (when taken in the context of what was said in Deuteronomy).

There is never a cut and dry or easy answer to whether a divorce is needed or not. Every situation has its own peculiarities. The purpose for this book is not to give a standard answer as to when a divorce is needed and when it is not. That is something about which each person will need to get direction from the Holy Spirit.

The thing I am trying to say is that the traditional view of divorce -- and often the subsequent remarriage -- is skewed at best, and wrong in many cases. Divorce is not what the church in general has said it is, nor does God view it like the church in general has viewed it. It is a much deeper subject than we have assumed. Because of the misunderstandings we've addressed, many honest, well-meaning people have been criticized, hurt, judged, condemned, and have left the church.

The church is often viewed as the enforcing officer of marriage, and you better not ever get a divorce if you want to be part of and accepted by the church. This is not right. How do I know that? Because the church is suppose to represent God on this earth, and God doesn't think that way. Who are we representing? Often, it's our own interests and beliefs.

10.) However, putting away and divorce do have further reaching consequences.

What do I mean by that? Most areas in which we are out of what God wants us to do (like lying, stealing, hate, fear, gossip, slander, betrayal, etc.) don't have as far-reaching of an impact as a marriage ending in divorce. No matter what area we are out of God's best, people will be hurt; but the devastation seems to be more widespread in marriage break-ups than in most other areas in which we mess up.

The partners are obviously affected the most; but right behind them are the children (if any are involved). From my experience, the children are typically affected for life if their parents divorce. It messes with their psyche, self-esteem, the role-modeled picture of what a father and mother are to look like, their picture of God, whether God is blamed for the marriage break-up, and on and on the list can go. However, I will agree that raising children in a severely dysfunctional family -- where mom and dad's relationship is a severe mess -- is not good for the them either. In fact, there are some cases where it's better for the children's sake if the couple divorces and moves on than continue in the dysfunction they are calling a family.

Let me give an example of that.

I know of situations where either the husband or the wife brought another man or woman into the home. By home, I don't mean house. I am saying they are brought into the marriage relationship as another partner. They may live under the same roof, or they may not. The new "partner" is equal with or even placed above the original spouse in that they are treated more like the marriage partner in every way -- including sexually -- than the original marriage partner. Neither the perpetrators, nor the legal system views it as polygamy, because they are not legally married to more than one partner. The original spouse has no say so in the matter. They can either agree to it, or get out.

In that situation, it's very obvious the victim has been put away for this new person. If that can't be fixed, my advice is to get out. Get your divorce and end it. The covenant is broken anyway, so let's set the victim free to move on and begin a new life with someone else if they choose. Interestingly enough, in one case I know of, that never happened. The "threesome" stayed in the same house and raised the children in that setting. It was a mess for the victimized spouse. It was also a mess for the children who had to grown up in it. It skewed the picture of God and every righteous thing that a marriage and family are

251

to represent. For the children's sake, it would have been better if those marriages had ended in divorce and the children grew up seeing a different picture than what they saw.

Let's go back to the original point of putting away and divorce having further-reaching consequences than other things. In a divorce situation, the extended family is also highly affected. Both individuals were loved and grew in various relationships in the family. Now, it's very difficult to keep those relationships intact. The church family is directly affected, because in a healthy church, both people in the marriage were loved. The people don't want to make a choice between one or the other. They loved both of them and their children and/or grand-children. Divorce causes a huge re-arrangement of what those relationships and interactions are going to look like. All the social relationships are put under strain and will have to adapt and change.

We haven't even addressed the financial, economic, and legal fallout, which also can be enormous.

Let's face it: divorce has far-reaching, devastating consequences, much more so than many other things we do.

11.) Why would God ever be in favor of a legal divorce?

We've discussed the first answer to that question in the last few points: to release the victim from a bad situation (Deuteronomy 22, 24; Matthew 5:31-32; 19:1-9; 1 Corinthians 7:10-16).

The second answer has to do with the individual, aside from the marriage. God's first love and priority has always been and will always be people. The various guidelines, rules, commands, and institutions that we find in scripture are all about helping people. Sometimes that is reversed, and we begin to think the reason we are alive is to fulfill all God's guidelines, rules, commands, and institutions. That is not God's heart. Every part of how God wants things run on earth is for the benefit of the human being.

This world in which we live is far from a perfect place, and despite our best efforts, people get hurt and damaged. We can make a bunch of rules to try to fix them, or we can actually care about the person. Rules tend to not fix people -- love does. Remember: love is not an absence of rules; it's prioritizing and ministering to what's most important. Once a person is hurt and damaged, they need room to heal before they are interested in or capable of restructuring their lives and priorities (rules). *That's another reason God made a way to get out of a bad marriage situation that isn't sin and doesn't heap a bunch of condemnation and guilt on the person. Very often, they are just trying to survive and preserve their life.*

> *Divorce is not what the church in general has said it is, nor does God view it like the church in general has viewed it.*

In an effort to preserve Godly morals and a base of morality, the church has established some traditions that are devastating to people. The institution of marriage and keeping everyone married (no matter how bad the marriage may be) is not worth destroying a person over. We may have our beliefs and doctrines in order, but we get so busy enforcing them that we lose sight of the fact that people are eternal souls. They can be hurt and damaged by the church and it's beliefs to the point they no longer want anything to do with God. We need to find a balance that retains the goal and focus of remaining married and making it a good marriage while still realizing that some marriages are going to crash and burn. We need to understand that not everybody that crashes and burns in their marriage is a "bad" person, nor should they now be kept at an arms length or restrained from doing anything important in the church.

Obviously there were issues in the couple's lives, or they could have worked through their marital problems. However, believe it or not, there are people who've been through a divorce -- maybe even precipitated it -- who do love God with everything within them. Again, in Christianity we tend to get things upside down. It should be love for God and His ways that motivate us to work on our weaknesses and get the sin out of our lives. Living free of sin in some area of our life is not proof we have this awesome love for God. All that proves is we're innocent of something. I know unbelievers who don't live in certain sins. That doesn't make them saved with a love for God. It merely makes them innocent in that area.

Everyone has strong areas, and we all have weak areas. My weaknesses may not be the same as someone else's, but I can guarantee you that we all have our areas.

> In some people, those weak areas cause business failure, for which they can declare bankruptcy and dissolve the company. It's completely legal and usually Ok with the church.

> Some weaknesses cause financial failure, for which one can go through a personal bankruptcy or foreclosure process. It's perfectly legal and usually Ok with the church and other Christians.

> Others weaknesses are the cause of someone dropping out of college, for which one can get a job or career without a college degree. This is legal, socially acceptable, and Ok with the church.

Some weaknesses cause injury and death through vehicle accidents, for which one has insurance and lawyers to help protect them in their bad decision. This also, even though unfortunate, is not a big issue with the church or most believers.

Some people struggle to remain drug free (whether prescribed or illegal), for which they can go to a treatment center, get sober and go on with life. This is also very acceptable by the church.

Other people's weaknesses cause them to struggle in maintaining a job or career for more than a few months or a year, for which they can receive counseling or therapy until their working life stabilizes. Usually the church is good with that too.

Other people's weaknesses cause them to lose their marriage, for which they can legally go to court and have the marriage dissolved in a righteous manner. However, this is completely unacceptable by most Christians and churches. In fact, in many churches, denominations, and believer's minds, there is no excuse -- period. They are now labeled, and there is no real way to be free of the stigma that was placed on them.

What's my point? Why does divorce carry a stigma for the remainder of the person's life, while other issues that develop from a person's weaknesses do not? Why do we as believers condemn one and often embrace the others? Chances are really good some form of sin was committed in every scenario listed above. Have we become hypocrites? Are we measuring right and wrong and then determining according to our standards what is OK and what is not?

Jesus didn't come to condemn the world, but to save it (John 3:17). The believer's and church's job is to help people overcome their weaknesses and the evil of this world. As Christians, and as the church, our

255

job is to help them, not judge, condemn, and discard them if they fail.

Many Christians have favorite quotes we hear from time to time. We say things like:

"The only failure is the person who doesn't get up a try again."

"In grace we can keep trying until we get it right."

"There is no limit to God's forgiveness."

"Overcoming often means trying to do it more than once."

"To overcome means you may not get it right on the first try."

"You may lose a battle or two before you are victorious."

And all of these are true in our minds, until we apply them to marriage. Just re-read the statements with marriage in mind. Now all of a sudden, they no longer apply. Let me just say it the way it is: that's hypocritical.

Let me give you an example, and just for the record -- my point here is not centered around protection, abstinence, etc. My point has to do with hypocrisy and destroying people for the sake of making ourselves look good or holding some standard. I know of many Christian marriage situations where porn is a normal part of the husband's or wife's life. If you don't believe me, just google the question of how many Christians are addicted to porn. The information is all at your fingertips. Technically speaking, that is fornication (we've already shown that in chapter 7). It is not something that God approves. The other partner is being put away for another man or woman, so the covenant has been broken. Yet, here is the average church's reasoning:

> "Well, the porn issue isn't right, but at least they're not
> divorced. They may have some problems, but at least
> they're still married."

Really? Married in whose opinion? God's, or ours?

I know this is the church's perspective. Let me ask a question: how many marriage retreats or classes does the average church have in comparison to the number of classes or retreats to deal with and get their people free from porn? In most churches, the subject of porn is never touched, when statistically there are more people in church who are addicted to porn than get divorced. Why don't we deal with porn? It's a sensitive subject. At the same time, we'll talk about how we shouldn't be divorced. Our thinking is somewhere in the realm of,

> "Well, the porn issue isn't right, but at least they're not
> divorced. They may have some problems, but at least
> they're still married."

God's interest isn't in keeping two people in the same house and filing the same tax return so it looks good in the church and community. In God's opinion, if they don't fix the problem, that covenant will be broken. If that happens, the marriage union is already over, just as if either partner had physically become involved with someone else in fornication. The scripture doesn't differentiate.

In our culture, porn seems to be more of a guy issue. However, statistically women are becoming more and more active in the porn scene. Since it is predominately more of a male issue, I'll address it from that perspective.

Many women have been counseled by the church to stay in relationships where the man has a full-out porn addiction. She is devastated.

She's struggling with emotional and self-esteem issues. She is trapped, controlled, and has no hope of life ever changing. Her questions will eventually turn to, "How God could be in favor of this?" because that's what the Christian pastor or counselor either insinuated or flat out said. The counsel she receives is that as long as they remain married, it's not a problem; every man has his needs. In many cases I've dealt with, the blame for the husband's problem was even put on her by the church because if she would do more to please him (especially sexually), he wouldn't have this problem. She becomes bitter with God, Christianity, the church, and other Christians. She begins to repel back from the very source from which she should be receiving her help. Why? Because of a bunch of man-made rules that will keep the family and church looking good in the eyes of others, at the expense of her devastation. She needs to "suck it up" and put up with it for the sake of the greater good which is staying in the marriage at any cost.

> *We need to understand that not everybody that crashes and burns in their marriage is a "bad" person.*

Guess what: in God's opinion, *she is the greater good.* God is not as interested in our reputations as He is interested in our eternal souls, and He will not trade a soul for a good reputation. He loves the person more than that.

If a marriage is a mess, let's do the best we can to get help and fix it!

If resolution doesn't take place, realize: we don't need to agree with what someone did to accept them and love them. Let's learn how to divide the behavior and performance away from the actual worth of the person. A human being's value and worth is not determined by their behavior and performance (e.g. whether or not we stayed married). Our value and worth is based on the fact we are created in the image and likeness of God. He loves us and saw us as worth giving His life for -- even when we were dead in sins and doing everything wrong. It's not our behavior that makes us valuable. It's the fact that we are created an eternal soul in the likeness of God that makes us more valuable than the whole world and everything in it.

12.) The Church's Traditional Viewpoint.

It's sad that the church of Jesus Christ has adopted a viewpoint that is not God's viewpoint in many cases. Much of the Christian community has taken an incorrect position on the subject. It's a posture and belief system that is different than what Jesus was teaching. Here are some of the key points that the church at large has adopted:

a.   God is against divorce. Divorce is sin. God hates divorce. Therefore to be divorced is to be viewed and often literally placed in a lower class of Christians. Often, certain jobs and positions within the church are no longer available to a divorced person. There is often an accompanying, devaluing attitude of: "Oh, you're divorced." It leaves the person with the feeling – "That's too bad; I feel sorry for you because you're less than the rest of us now." It's the feeling that somehow they are now damaged beyond God's ability to truly repair and restore them fully.

b.   A second viewpoint is that divorce is forbidden, except if there has been proven or admitted adultery (fornication). If there has been fornication or adultery, then God is OK with the divorce and moving on. Anything beyond that is sin and inexcusable.

c. A divorced person is not allowed to remarry, especially if the reason for the divorce was not adultery or fornication. If they do, they will always be living in adultery with their new partner.

d. A person who has been divorced can never be in the ministry (licensed or ordained as a deacon or minister). In fact, in many churches, they can never serve again unless they are doing something that is viewed as fairly menial. They are no longer worthy of holding an important position or office. This is usually because we wouldn't want to set a bad example; or it's the belief that divorce (and especially remarriage) is an ongoing sin, and a sinner shouldn't be ministering.

Yet from the minister, on down through the board, members, teachers, etc. -- there are numerous marriages where one or the other has been put away. They treat each other badly. The bond of oneness is obviously gone. Apparently, that doesn't make any difference, as long as they don't get legally divorced.

Once we understand what the scripture really says about these subjects, it's fairly easy to see how those conclusions are not correct. In fact, they are hypocritical.

13.) What if we were both believers when we ended our marriage?

The only passage of scripture we've looked at that differentiates between believers and unbelievers in this process is where Paul explains it in 1 Corinthians 7.

To answer the question, all the same principles apply whether one is a believer or both. If one or both of the people in the marriage are so hard-hearted that they cannot reconcile their differences, one or both are being violated and abused. They have set their jaw, and they are not going to change. In these cases, it may be better for all involved if the marriage was legally ended. The covenant has very, very likely been broken long ago. The sin is also the same in all cases -- it's the putting away that has taken place because of hard hearts that is the sin.

14.) What about ministry after divorce and/or remarriage?

Let's look at what the scripture says about that issue. Most of the time the first passages that are brought up are 1 Timothy 3 and Titus 1. Let's look at them.

1 Timothy 3:1-2 (NIV - underline added)
[1] Here is a trustworthy saying: If anyone sets his heart on being an overseer, he desires a noble task. [2] Now the overseer must be above reproach, the husband of but one wife, temperate, self-controlled, respectable, hospitable, able to teach,

1 Timothy 3:12 (NIV - underline added)
[12] A deacon must be the husband of but one wife and must manage his children and his household well.

Titus 1:5-6 (NIV - underline added)
[5] The reason I left you in Crete was that you might straighten out what was left unfinished and appoint elders in every town, as I directed you. [6] An elder must be blameless, the husband of but one wife, a man whose children believe and are not open to the charge of being wild and disobedient.

The direct Greek translation of this phrase would read: an elder must be *"a one woman kind of guy,"* or a *"one woman man."*

What is the Holy Spirit saying through Paul? Let's first look at what He CAN'T be saying.

a. To be an elder or a deacon, you must be married. That would disqualify anyone who is single or not married. Even though the wording makes it sound that way -- "A deacon must be the husband of but one wife" -- this can't be saying you must be married to be in the ministry. Why? Jesus (the Lord of the Church) would be disqualified. He was never married while on earth. To our knowledge, when Paul was in ministry, he wasn't married either. Nor is there evidence that a number other ministers in the New Testament were ever married. So if being married is a qualification, a number of the New Testament ministers are disqualified.

b. It can't be talking about a person who has been divorced. If it were, it would exclude God Himself from ever ministering to someone. Why? He's divorced.

c. If someone is divorced and remarried, do they now have more than one wife or husband? According to Deut. 24:1-4 -- and Jesus' reaffirmation of that position in Matt. 5:31-32, 19:8-9, Mark 10:11-12, and Luke 16:18 where Jesus is upholding and giving clarification on Deut. 24 -- if a person does what God commanded and actually gives a bill of divorce and not just put the spouse away, they are no longer considered married. That's why God did that with Israel in Jeremiah 3. That way, He would no longer be married to her.

The point is that if a couple goes through the correct legal process of filing the paperwork with the courts ("writing of divorce"), they are no longer married. They are considered single. Whether they remain single or get remarried, they are no longer married to the former spouse. Conclusion: a remarried person is only married to one person.

So what IS the Holy Spirit saying?

a. What would Paul be talking about? He's addressing the

problem of his day, which, by the way, had been a problem for hundreds if not thousands of years. The problem was polygamy. Because of the culture of paganism in which Paul ministered, I'm quite certain some of Paul's converts had multiple wives, concubines, and maybe even wives who had been put away but not divorced. It was an issue that had to be dealt with in the church so the abuses of women that were happening in the Old Testament and in society would not continue on in the New Testament church.

Paul is saying that men and women are not allowed in the bishop or deacon offices if they have multiple partners (simultaneously married to more than one person). This was common in the time Paul was writing to Timothy and Titus. It is still common in parts of the world.

I have been confronted with polygamy in counseling settings. However, in most of the cases, there was only one wife living in America. The other wives lived in other parts of the world. Polygamy is still a fairly common practice, depending on which present day country and culture to which you are referring.

Let's answer the question: what about ministry after divorce and/or remarriage? Scripturally that doesn't seem to be a concern to God. Credibility, reputation, and current behavior are of greater concern to God. There is nothing in scripture that indicates a divorced and/or a divorced and remarried person cannot be in the ministry. But like some other things, tradition and rules of men have made divorce and remarriage one of the worst things in which a person can be involved. From God's perspective, He doesn't always see it like we see it. Nothing seems to change with mankind. Just like in Jesus' day, we strain gnats, but swallow camels (Matt. 23:24). Just like with the teachers of the law and the Pharisees, the more important things like justice, mercy, and faithfulness can be overlooked. We need to remember that the person or people are eternally more important than the institution and handle them accordingly.

263

What if I'm Guilty

Chapter 9

What should I do if unfortunately I have either put away a spouse or have been put away by a spouse, and I have been legally divorced? What Should I do? How should I look at this?

If it is still in the put away phase, seek help. Get the problems fixed so your marriage can remain intact and be a good, Godly marriage. It is still very much fixable. Deal with the hard heart issues in both spouses. Make reconciliation and restoration the highest priority.

If it's past that, and you're already divorced: begin by asking God to forgive you for anything that may have happened that wasn't right. The most important thing is to make sure you are right with God. He's the One to whom we will answer for what happened in our life on this earth. Make sure you have everything taken care of with Him.

Next: forgive yourself for anything that may have happened that wasn't right. You need to be able to unhook from your past and move on. If you don't, it will become a ball and chain around any forward progress for the rest of your life. It's over, and in most cases there is nothing that can be done to change that. If you haven't done it yet, it's time to let God's forgiveness and grace set you free to have a productive future.

Then: forgive the other person. Make the choice to verbally release them from any ill will, bad feelings, blame, desire for revenge or punishment, or wishing bad into their life. Any unforgiveness you carry toward them will only paralyze you and jeopardize your relationship with God.

Remember the Lord's Prayer:

Matthew 6:9-15 (NIV - underline added)
[9] "This, then, is how you should pray: " 'Our Father in heaven, hallowed be your name, [10] your kingdom come, your will be done on earth as it is in heaven. [11] Give us today our daily bread. [12] Forgive us our debts, as we also have forgiven our debtors. [13] And lead us not into temptation, but deliver us from the evil one.' [14] For if you forgive men when they sin against you, your heavenly Father will also forgive you. [15] But if you do not forgive men their sins, your Father will not forgive your sins.

Verse 12 asks God to forgive our sins as we have forgiven those who sin against us.

Then in v. 14-15, Jesus wanted to be sure that we understood: if we forgive others, we will be forgiven. If we do not forgive others, we will not be forgiven. That's nothing to mess around with. That can affect our eternal future. It's better to just do what's right and forgive them.

Next: I would recommend asking their forgiveness. You can do this through a letter, phone call, or in person. If nothing else, it values them and restores a dignity to them like few other things you could say or do. It also is an expression of respect and love for them as a fellow human being.

Lastly: In the cases where the former relationship can be reconciled, make the effort to do so. If not, move on in life without condemnation.

The good news is, God forgives and He forgets (Hebrews 8:12, 10:17). Even if you were totally at fault in the putting away and divorce -- if we ask, God forgives and He forgets. Divorce is not the unpardonable sin. It can be forgiven. It's time to move on in life and quit second-guessing yourself. Realize you haven't lost any value, worth, or usefulness to God. He loves you as much as He did before the divorce. You are not a second-rate citizen in His opinion. In fact, if you bring it up to Him, He may say, "I have no memory of what you are talking about". When He forgave, He chose to let it go and forget it.

You are still a valuable member of His family and His kingdom.

Chances are really good that what happened hasn't bothered anyone else as much as it has bothered the two of you who were involved with the break-up. Now it's time to let go of it and move on.

Remember: God is not as quick to condemn as man is, and His opinion on the situation is the one that matters the most.

> *Realize you haven't lost any value, worth, or usefulness to God.*
>
> *He loves you as much as He did before the divorce.*

Remarriage

Chapter 10

Is it Ok to remarry?

Does God feel "divorce" and "remarriage" are all right? Absolutely, under certain circumstances. But remember, if He had his way with the human race, we wouldn't be having this discussion; this world would have gone a whole different direction. But sin did enter the human race, and as a result of that, there are many things that God did not originally intend for us to have to deal with. Putting away, divorce, and remarriage are among them.

With that said, God is a realist and knows that "it is what it is". Let's deal with it and make something good out of this mess. The best proof of that is found in God sending His son to die on the cross so He could make good come out of a very bad situation. God is viewing it as, "Here's what's real; let's deal with it."

God realizes we are living in an imperfect world, and bad things are going to happen. Let's deal with them and move on. God made it clear that it is permissible to remarry after a divorce. He said it in three different places.

Dt 24:1-2 (KJV - underline added)
[1] When a man hath taken a wife, and married her, and it come to

pass that she find no favour in his eyes, because he hath found some uncleanness in her: then let him write her a bill of divorcement, and give it in her hand, and send her out of his house.
[2] And when she is departed out of his house, she may go and be another man's wife.

Matthew 19:1-9 (KJV - underline added)
[1] And it came to pass, that when Jesus had finished these sayings, he departed from Galilee, and came into the coasts of Judaea beyond Jordan; [2] And great multitudes followed him; and he healed them there. [3] The Pharisees also came unto him, tempting him, and saying unto him, "Is it lawful for a man to put away his wife for every cause?" [4] And he answered and said unto them, "Have ye not read, that he which made them at the beginning made them male and female, [5] And said, For this cause shall a man leave father and mother, and shall cleave to his wife: and they twain shall be one flesh? [6] Wherefore they are no more twain, but one flesh. What therefore God hath joined together, let not man put asunder." [7] They say unto him, "Why did Moses then command to give a writing of divorcement, and to put her away?" [8] He saith unto them, "Moses because of the hardness of your hearts suffered you to put away your wives: but from the beginning it was not so. [9] And I say unto you, Whosoever shall put away his wife, except it be for fornication, and shall marry another, committeth adultery: and whoso marrieth her which is put away doth commit adultery."

At first glance it may seem like the verses in Matthew aren't addressing remarriage, but they are. Jesus is addressing the situation of remarriage from the perspective that they took for granted they may remarry (He refers to it twice in verse 19). Remember: the Pharisees were questioning him about Deuteronomy 24:1-2 (above). He's answering them. Deuteronomy 24 definitely says a person can remarry. Jesus isn't contradicting that, but He is giving the guidelines on how it should play out.

Remember, in their culture, they had a problem with polygamy and simply putting a wife away for another wife, but not giving the first wife a legal divorce. This caused her to be trapped in a hopeless situation. If she tried to remarry, she would be in adultery. Now notice something. Read v. 9 of Matthew 19 very closely. The Pharisees liked to put the whole adultery on the woman. But Jesus just put it back on them.

> "Whosoever shall put away his wife… and shall marry another, committeth adultery."

Jesus is saying, Guys this isn't all about the woman. If you do this the wrong way and you marry another, YOU will be committing adultery also. I'm sure that was news to them.

Jesus is talking about remarriage. He's not saying it's a sin. He is saying there is a specific way it needs to be done.

Jesus had to be in agreement with Deuteronomy 24, or He would have been breaking the law. That would have made Him a sinner, and He would no longer have been qualified to be our Savior.

He's not against remarriage. In fact, in v. 9 it appears as if He is assuming it will happen. Remarriage is going to happen, and He says nothing to indicate that the remarriage is wrong. What is wrong is if the putting away is handled incorrectly. (For a full explanation of this passage, please see chapter 7.)

Because Jesus is answering the question they asked (v. 7) and is referring to that same verse (Deuteronomy 24:1-2) in His answer, He's in agreement with Deut. 24 when it says,"when she is departed out of his house, she may go and be another man's wife." That's why He answers the question as if He's taking it for granted someone will remarry.

Paul also directly addressed remarriage in 1 Corinthians 7:27-28.

1 Corinthians 7:27-28 (KJV - underline added)
[27] Art thou bound unto a wife? seek not to be loosed. Art thou loosed
from a wife? seek not a wife.
[28] But and if thou marry, thou hast not sinned; and if a virgin marry,
she hath not sinned....

The word "bound" here is the same one we looked at in 1 Corinthians 7:39 and Romans 7:2 (See chapter 7 for full details). Being "bound" to a wife or husband is talking about being married.

The word "loosed" is "luo" in the Greek. It means to be "released, untied, unbound." Every time this Greek word is used, it refers to something that had been intact at one time, but has been dissolved or broken in pieces.

Let's put those two words into these scriptures. Paul was sharing his opinion (v. 12, 25, 40) on what was the best thing to do considering the crisis they were in during that time (Paul referred to the crisis in 1 Corinthians 7).

Here is what those scriptures are saying if you put the original Greek definitions for "bound" and "loosed" into them:

v. 27 - If you already HAVE a wife, don't look for a way to be released from or untied from her and the marriage (legally divorced). If you HAD a wife, but you have been "loosed" from her and the marriage (either legally divorced or the spouse had died), don't get married again.

v. 28 - However, (if the person WAS divorced, or their husband HAD died -- v. 27) if you DO REMARRY, you have not sinned. And if someone gets married who was never married before, they have not sinned.

Paul is talking about divorce, remarriage, and a first time marriage in these two scriptures. There are three different groups of people being addressed. To understand these two scriptures, you need to see that.

v. 27a - a married person.

v. 27b - a divorced person, or someone whose spouse had died.

v. 28a - a divorced person, or someone whose spouse had died.

v. 28b - someone who has never been married.

The point that fits this discussion is this: if you're divorced, you are not sinning if you remarry.

So, can a person remarry after they have been divorced? According to the Bible, yes.

God realizes we are living in an imperfect world and bad things are going to happen. Let's deal with them and move on.

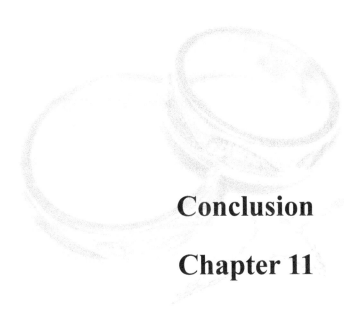

Conclusion

Chapter 11

I'd like to repeat something I said at the beginning of the book.

I have hesitated to write this book because of my concern that people will simply use the material to justify what they've wanted to do all along -- find a way out of their marriage and still be Ok with God. I pray that does not happen, because that's neither what I, nor the scriptures, are saying.

To my knowledge, there has never been a case where both of the spouses were walking in love toward each other, and they still divorced. The solution to the issue is not difficult; however -- no matter how easy the solution may be -- people still put each other away and divorce.

God intended the marriage covenant to be a life-long commitment and agreement. We've seen where He said that when He joined two people together, man was never to separate them. I realize there may be other factors and issues involved with various marriage situations, but from my perspective, the basic reason a marriage falls apart is exactly what Jesus said: it's the hardness of the hearts of one or both of the partners. When our hearts are hard or calloused to spiritual things, a number of things are immediately affected. We're unable to experience or express genuine (agape) love for our spouse. Once that type of Godly Love is removed from the equation, everything else that creates a lasting bond between people is soon in shambles. Patience disappears, understanding is gone, empathy does not exist, the desire to invest into the other person dries up, and pretty much everything that creates the glue or bond that holds people together in any framework simply dies. Now, all that remains is selfishness, looking out for one's self, taking care of their own desires and needs above anyone else's, and disregard for another's thinking, emotions, welfare, and future life.

It's the spiritually hard heart that kills the marriage.

Make no mistake about it, Jesus said marriages fail because of the hard heart of one or both of the spouses. So if a marriage fails after reading this book, it's not the books' fault. It's the hard hearts of the people in the marriage. Some may say, "But they stayed married until they read this book, and you gave them permission to get divorced. It's your fault."

My response to that is as follows:

    a. People don't get divorced unless someone has already been put away. Their problems were in existence before they found this book.

    b. If the marriage was so bad that it only took a little new information to cause the divorce -- then were they still married in God's sight, or only man's? Remember: there is a difference.

    c. The reason for the divorce is the hard heart of one or both of the spouses. They simply chose not to fix it.

d. When a person is already wanting to do something in their heart, any excuse will do. This book didn't cause their heart issue -- it revealed it.

The only remedy for a hard heart that can save a marriage is true, honest interactions with God that will change the person at their core. It will soften the deep-seated, selfish ungodliness that is ruling in the person's heart and life. Once a person's heart is revitalized, new information and a new understanding of how the covenant of marriage is to be handled will be necessary. It's the old information that helped cause the problem. So get help. Seek spiritual help, and seek life-changing encounters with God. Then, find and devour information so you can gain a new knowledge of how a Godly marriage is to be formed and what principles it must be built upon to run smoothly for everyone involved.

Remember: It is the hard heart problem that is the core of faltering marriages. It is alive and healthy in relationships where one or both don't want to change. They like who and what they are, even if it is destroying the marriage. They refuse help. They resist most any input that could help them and their situation. They avoid or even run from people and situations that would honestly desire to simply help them. Their mind is made up and their attitudes are set. They refuse to waver from the path on which they are running their life.

To my knowledge, there has never been a case where both of the spouses were walking in love toward each other, and they still divorced.

In those settings, a marriage will really struggle to survive. Almost inevitably, one person is the perpetrator and the

277

other is the victim. One spouse takes the parent role, while the other is forced into the child's role. Verbal, emotional, or even physical abuse is always present. One or both partners are acting violently toward the other. That often includes numerous elements, such as criticism, put-downs, belittling, control, anger, bitterness, unforgiveness, stone-walling, neglect, cussing and swearing at the other, lying, cheating, threats, affairs, and on the list can go.

This is not what a marriage was designed to be. This couple needs help. They should seek help and change what is happening. But what if one or both refuse to seek help? From my experience, it's typically one person who digs in their heels and refuses to get counsel or help. In my opinion, this makes the situation even worse because the other spouse is going to be abused and covered with violence against them. They are suffering. They are trapped in a horrible situation where they are no longer the priority -- they're no longer number one. They are living off the emotional and sometimes physical scraps that the abuser gives them. They have been put away. If children are involved, they are also suffering.

Should they stay living in that situation? I don't have a general, one-size-fits-all answer for that. Ultimately, you will need to receive your answer from God. He is the one who knows the situation and hearts better than anyone. He is the one to whom you will ultimately answer. He will tell you what to do.

We looked at God's principles on these types of situations. He has made a way out of broken marriages where someone has been put away. You will need to make the final decision, and I would recommend the strongest input on that decision come from Him.

However, in those bad, ungodly situations, divorce is a privilege. It was given as a solution to some very intolerable abuses and violations (which God evidently considers worse). I would like to say that the decision should be made with extreme caution. Just like so many privileges, it is taken advantage of. Often, the couple takes the avenue of divorce when they shouldn't have. When they do, it always happens because of hard hearts. Like Jesus said, "From the beginning it was not so."

Yet, when the situation sincerely warrants a divorce, in God's opinion, it is a solution to some disgusting and abhorring situations. In comparison to being put away, a written divorce offers a realm of human dignity for the partner from whom it is being stripped by the behavior of the hard-hearted spouse. It ends a bad situation and offers the victim a way to get out and start over -- with God's approval.

Through being put away, abandoned, deserted, or however it is described, the hard-hearted perpetrator literally controls and destroys the victim's life. This has been and is forbidden by God, the Law, and Jesus.

Even with that knowledge and understanding of how God looks at the breaking of a covenant and divorce, move with extreme caution. It's easy to justify ourselves and convince ourselves that we are doing the right thing by getting a divorce. Make sure you know that you know there is no other solution. Make certain you aren't just taking the easy way out, when in reality what one or both partners need to do is not get divorced, but get over their selfishness and grow up.

Guys, whatever you do, pay attention to how you handle your wife. God does protect the woman who has been put away. Let me give two more scriptures that show this.

Exodus 21:7-11 (NIV)
[7] "If a man sells his daughter as a servant, <u>she is not to go free as</u>

279

menservants do. [8] If she does not please the master who has selected her for himself, he must let her be redeemed. He has no right to sell her to foreigners, because he has broken faith with her. [9] If he selects her for his son, he must grant her the rights of a daughter. [10] If he marries another woman, he must not deprive the first one of her food, clothing and marital rights. [11] If he does not provide her with these three things, she is to go free, without any payment of money.

Overlook the cultural aspects of selling daughters. I know it's repulsive, but that's the way it was. What I want you to notice is that in the middle of all this stuff that happened at the expense of the women, God still set limits in what could be done. Why? To protect the women.

In this scripture, God says if you're going to buy someone as a servant or wife, you will take care of her correctly and treat her well. If you don't, she has the right to go free, and doesn't have to pay back any of the money you gave when you bought her. She owes you nothing because of what you did to her. "To go free" means she is able to start over in life, marry whomever she will, and God is in favor of it.

He says basically the same thing about a different situation in Deuteronomy:

Deuteronomy 21:10-14 (AMP)
[10] When you go forth to battle against your enemies and the Lord your God has given them into your hands and you carry them away captive, [11] And you see among the captives a beautiful woman and desire her, that you may have her as your wife, [12] Then you shall bring her home to your house, and she shall shave her head and pare her nails [in purification from heathenism] [13] And put off her prisoner's garb, and shall remain in your house and bewail her father and her mother a full month. After that you may go in to her and be her hus

band and she shall be your wife. [14] And if you have no delight in her, then you shall let her go absolutely free. You shall not sell her at all for money; you shall not deal with her as a slave or a servant, because you have humbled her.

In this situation, God is stepping up to protect a woman from another nation who is actually a heathen nation (v. 12). If she is not being treated correctly, He says she must be set free, just like in the last scripture we read in Exodus 21.

God hates the mistreatment of women, especially in the marriage setting. In both of these scriptures, He has made it clear that He'd sooner see the woman go free (divorced so she can go on in life) than to remain in a situation where she is being disdained and violated.

For those who are either in a broken covenant marriage, or you've already come through the process and are divorced, there are a few things I think it is imperative you realize:

1.) <u>God still loves you.</u> Whatever happened has not changed how God feels about you and the fact that you are still loved by Him. His love is unconditional, and how much He loves you does not depend on your performance.

2.) <u>He's not out to get you now.</u> <u>He doesn't wish you harm or evil.</u> <u>He doesn't hate you.</u> You haven't so totally disappointed Him that there is no hope of ever gaining His acceptance. He is waiting with open arms to be your friend, helper, and guide through this and for the rest of your life.

3.) <u>Life goes on after divorce, even for Christians.</u> I know that may sound odd, because if life is available to anyone, it is especially for believers (John 10:10). Yet the way I worded it is still true: life goes on after divorce, even for Christians. The reason I say it that way is because, depending upon what kind of religious climate to which you have been exposed, you have been taught that divorce is one of the greatest sins that could ever be committed. Now you are loaded down with guilt, shame, and confusion. You feel (and maybe actually are) isolated from most or all of your Christian friends. You feel (and maybe actually are) judged by the church and the community of people with whom you once had a close relationship. You feel like a failure and like you've let everyone down. You feel (and maybe are) alone, not knowing what to really think or with whom you can even talk who will give you an honest, loving, Godly reality check.

Realize something: Jesus said He'd never leave you nor forsake you. People may, but He won't. Take your eyes off of people and their opinions and feelings, and put your eyes on God. Go to Jesus and pour your heart out to Him. Tell him everything that is going on inside of you, and ask Him to help you. He will. *He will*. *He loves you more than you can imagine, and He grieves as He watches you suffer*. If anyone will accept you exactly as you are without putting on pretense or playing a role, it is God. Just be real with Him, and ask Him to be real with you. He will meet you and walk you through this.

4.) <u>There will be a long process of healing from the wounds that the bad marriage inflicted. Don't rush the healing process.</u> There will be several stages through which you will walk to get healthy again. Let them play out without rushing them or simply skipping them.

Too many people rush this process or "rebound" from the deep hurt of having been put away and divorced. As a result, they make some bad decisions and ultimately create a bigger mess. Don't do that. Give yourself time to heal and gain new information and insight before you move on. Remember, something went horribly wrong the first time.

Do you best to prevent it from happening again.

Many refer to the first part of this healing time as the stages of grief. Here is a list of them.

Shock and Denial (mental reaction)
Pain and Guilt (emotional reaction)
Anger and Bargaining (first effort at resolution)
Depression and Loneliness (realization of situation)
Acceptance and New Focus (taking a turn toward recovery)
Resolution (rebuilding for future)

Again I encourage you, seek Godly counsel to help you walk through them. And may I qualify what I mean by Godly? I mean someone who honestly is loving and serving God with all their heart and DOES NOT focus on how wrong you were for destroying your marriage or push you to go back and fix it immediately.

Here is God's heart on the matter: whether the marriage is ever restored or not depends on two people -- you and your former spouse. Both of you will need to focus on yourselves and heal. Become healthy before attempting any type of restoration. Right now, there is likely far too much damage for that relationship to come back together and be anything other than what it was before you divorced. If the marriage is never restored, life goes on after divorce. You need to heal and become healthy so that your life can be good once again.

Give that process the time it needs so that God can heal you.

5.) This may sound odd coming from a minister, but my advice is to avoid the people who are against you, condemning your actions, judging you, and somehow letting you know you messed up and are a failure. It doesn't matter if they call themselves Christians or not, this is not a representation of the heart of God. Let me share with you the heart of God and how He deals with someone who is wounded and struggling:

Matthew 12:20-21 (AMP)
[20] A bruised reed He will not break, and a smoldering (dimly burning) wick He will not quench, till He brings justice and a just cause to victory. [21] And in and on His name will the Gentiles (the peoples outside of Israel) set their hopes.

This is found in a section of scripture that talks about the characteristics of Jesus and how He handles people.

When we are bruised, He doesn't come into our situation and break us. If the light of life and hope is barely flickering in us, He doesn't snuff it out. He will work with us where we are at. He will work with you where you are at right now. His goal is always the same: to make sure justice and the just cause wins out in the end. He will bring justice into your life and situation. That's why the people of the earth set their hopes on Him. It's because of what He is like.

Jesus is not like many of the people who claim they are serving Him. Christians can tend to be very self-righteous and condemning. If you want healing, you may need to avoid that type of person until you have reached a point of health where what they say and how they may look at you or make you feel no longer has a negative affect on you.

6.) Above all, guard your heart so that the poisonous seed of blaming

God cannot take root. If it is already growing and producing poison in your heart and attitudes toward God, pull it out. Kill it.

What happened to you is not God's fault.   If there is anyone in your corner, wanting to make sure you come through this and working to keep it from destroying you, it's God.

God gave mankind the right to run their own life and make their own decisions. It's called a free will. God rarely over-rules that original design of free will. A person chose to do this to you and the relationship. *It wasn't God's choice, and it isn't His fault.*

I've heard many people express how crushed and disappointed they are in God, because they prayed, asked, and begged Him to do something to stop the abuse and violence; to do something about all the bad things that were happening; to come and protect them, or rescue them; and He did nothing. They felt abandoned and betrayed by the one in whom they trusted the most -- God. Now they are fighting with being bitter, angry, and resentful towards God.

If you let those thoughts, feelings, and attitudes continue to fester in you, it will separate you from God. Don't let that happen. He's not your problem.

> *A person chose to do this to you*
> *and the relationship.*
>
> *It wasn't God's choice, and it isn't His fault.*

The last point I'd like to address is the children. If children are involved with the broken marriage and divorce, don't ignore them and their pain. Adults often feel overwhelmed by what just happened, and we typically have greater reasoning and comprehending abilities than children. The advent of a broken marriage and subsequent divorce can literally drown a child in mental confusion and negative emotions.

I realize as the damaged partner of a divorce, you are trying to survive; but so are they. The divorce damaged them also.

I'm not going to say a lot about this point, but that doesn't diminish its importance. Don't ignore the needs of your children. They won't just somehow survive this thing undamaged. They need help, too.

1.) <u>They are in desperate need of stability.</u> Everything in their life has become very unstable. The healthy and stable relationships that remain in your life are a gift to you. I realize many people have abandoned you through the situation, but not everybody. There will be some people who are Godly and mature enough to stick with you and help you through this process. Utilize the help they are offering to you, especially if they have a connection with and positive affect on your children.

2.) <u>They are in desperate need of understanding.</u> At best, they are struggling to comprehend what just happened to their world. They don't get it. Someone with the skills and abilities to work with them in a positive manner needs to help them. I realize the parent with whom they are living is extremely vital in helping them with this, but remember: you are likely in survival mode yourself, and any insight you may have to give will likely be skewed right now. Bring someone into the situation and their lives who has a Godly understanding of what has happened and the ability to connect with them mentally and emotionally. They need help, too. If they don't get that help -- no matter how good they may appear to be handling it on the outside -- the family breakup and divorce will cause catastrophic damage on the inside. They need help working through that.

Hopefully you can find some encouragement when you realize how God really feels about the pain and suffering you are going through, or have gone through. You are of more value to Him than all the rules and regulations you been told are "really important" to God. Jesus didn't die so rules and regulations could be upheld. Jesus died for people. He came for you.

His perspective on divorce and remarriage is not nearly as harsh as it has been taught. His love for the person -- for you -- shows up all the way through the Bible. He is not as quick to condemn as people or the church can be.

Look at one more scripture with me:

Isaiah 54:4-6 (NIV)
[4] "Do not be afraid; you will not suffer shame. Do not fear disgrace; you will not be humiliated. You will forget the shame of your youth and remember no more the reproach of your widowhood. [5] For your Maker is your husband—the LORD Almighty is his name—the Holy One of Israel is your Redeemer; he is called the God of all the earth. [6] The LORD will call you back as if you were a wife deserted and distressed in spirit—a wife who married young, only to be rejected," says your God.

Here God is talking about a woman who is afraid, filled with shame, and afraid of further disgrace and humiliation (v. 4a). God promises that He will help her forget the shame of the things that happened when she was young and the reproach of her "widowhood" (v. 4b). This woman is in a bad way. Whatever has happened to her really messed her up. So what happened? It's all wrapped in the word "widowhood."

"Widowhood" can mean two things:

    1.) It can mean, "a woman whose husband has died."

That in and of itself would not produce the deep wounds and scars this woman has. But there is a second meaning to that word which would fit the description much better.

    2.) It can mean, "someone who was deserted or forsaken by a husband; discarded as a divorced person." It's referring to someone who was "put away".

That would fit the description that God gave of this person: afraid, suffering, shameful, afraid the disgrace and humiliation will continue. It also makes more sense with v. 5 & 6 in which God says, "I am your Maker, and I will be your husband." He will call her back as a deserted, forsaken, and distressed woman, grieved to the deepest core -- in her spirit. "A woman who married young, but was then rejected," goes along with the concept of being "put away". This is how the Amplified states verse 6:

Isaiah 54:6 (AMP)
[6] For the Lord has called you like a woman forsaken, grieved in spirit, and heartsore -- even a wife [wooed and won] in youth, when she is [later] refused and scorned, says your God.

She was destroyed by the previous husband, but she is about to be rescued by God Himself, and He wants to take care of her like her husband should have.

Who is this God? He gives three of his names to back up what he just said:

1.) "The Lord Almighty is his name." This again is "Jehovah-Tsaba," "the God of war, service, and the appointed time." He will go to war, if needed, to set this woman free. He is her defender, as any good husband should be. This is speaking of the Father.

2.) "The Holy One of Israel, your Redeemer." This is a name that refers to Jesus. He's the Redeemer. He will buy the woman back from this situation, re-"deem" her and restore her, no matter what that may cost.

3.) "The God of all the earth." "God" here is the name "Elohim". This is the name that refers to God as the Creator (the name used in Genesis chapters 1 & 2). It speaks of His complete power, might, creative ability and power, and complete sovereignty. It is also the name that is defined as "Gods" (the Trinity). This is the God who looks at this woman's situation and says, "If there is no way out or solution for her, I'll create one. It doesn't matter what anyone may say or think -- I'm Sovereign over her." Because of the name "Elohim," we know this includes the Holy Spirit.

Wow! This is amazing! Talk about riding in on a white horse to rescue this woman. The Father, The Son, and the Holy Spirit are in on rescuing her.

Who is she? Someone who has been crushed by her husband, deserted, cast away, forsaken, discarded, afraid, suffering, shameful, grieved, disgraced, and distressed -- a good description of a horrible "putting away". God says, "I will be the husband you didn't have, and I'll defend you and take care of you."

Who is this? It's a put away woman who is about to be remarried to God Himself.

Don't tell me that God isn't concerned with people who have been damaged by broken marriages. The entire Godhead (Trinity) gets involved to help and rescue them. There are no lengths that God will not go to in order to help a put away, divorced person (especially if that person has been an abused woman).

God is quick to share His compassion, grace, and mercy for those who have been put away and divorced. The church and other believers need to understand: that is the heart of God for someone who has been crushed by a bad marriage. Our goal should be to emulate Him rather than judge, condemn, and distance ourselves from them because they're divorced.

I am not encouraging divorce or agreeing with a cop-out, but we need to minister grace and love to people and learn to see them as God does.

My Prayer is that this book will be of help and give hope to those who need it the most. If that's you, my heart goes out to you. The pain you have suffered is probably indescribable. Hopefully, now that you see what God really feels about you and what happened, you can find peace and move on in life.

If that isn't you, now that you understand some things about covenant, putting away, and divorce that you probably didn't realize before, please help the person who's struggling in a bad marriage. There are many people in our society and churches who have been put away by their spouse. Help them to see that God is not in favor of what is going on, and He doesn't condone it.

You now have some comfort that you can give to the person who has been damaged and wounded by a divorce. You see the heart of God and what He feels for them, as well as how He views the divorce that took place.

Again, thank you for reading this book. My hope is that it will somehow help you in your life.

Vern

> *God loves the individual far more*
> *than the rule or regulation.*
>
> *If forced to choose, He will*
> *always choose the person.*

Contact Information:

Vern Peltz
wordoflifemn.org

Made in USA - North Chelmsford, MA
1365627_9781979198530
04.03.2023 1056